The Lawyer's Ultimate Guide to Online Leads

2018 Edition

Fourth edition: February 2018

Printed in the United States of America

ISBN: 978-0-9861613-0-8

Updates

To get updates to this book, to access new videos and to speak directly with the author, Ken Matejka, please contact us.

- Email: info@matejkamarketing.com
- Phone: (415) 513-8736
- Website: www.matejkamarketing.com

The Lawyer's Ultimate Guide to Online Leads

2018 Edition

Getting More Online Clients into Your Law Practice, Step-By-Step

Ken Matejka, J.D., LL.M.

Table of Contents

What's New in the 2018 Edition?

Here are some of the highlights of what's different from the 2017 version of this book:

- Google started recording phone calls that originate through a Google ad in November 2017 ostensibly for "quality assurance" and to "prevent fraud", possibly compromising the attorney-client privilege.

- Under the guise of giving its advertisers "more flexibility," in October 2017, Google decided that it was OK to spend up to 200% of our daily advertising budget.

- More on Yelp and its recent crackdown on the solicitation of reviews.

- There's a new chapter on reputation management as it becomes an increasing concern for lawyers with negative content about them in Google's search results.

- Facebook finally enters the find-a-local-business market with "Facebook Local."

- In the summer of 2017, Google started serving up different maps search results when consumers added a superlative like "best lawyers," apparently based upon the number of 5-star Google+ reviews.

- Avvo's "Marketing Fee" that it charges lawyers is found to be an illegal fee split by several states.

- The ABA updated it's stance from a 1999 formal opinion relating to the use of unencrypted email for transmission of confidential client information.

If you bought an earlier edition of this book, write to info@matejkamarketing.com and I'll email this updated edition to you as a pdf.

About the Author

Ken Matejka (J.D., LL.M in Taxation) has been a California attorney for 29 years and is a former-member of the American Bar Association's Standing Committee on Lawyer Referral and Information Services.

For 17 years, he worked at the Lawyer Referral and Information Service of the Bar Association of San Francisco and for many years there, as LRIS Operations Manager, he was chiefly responsible for advertising the LRIS, including actively managing its Google advertising.

In 2007, he left the Bar Association of San Francisco to found a search engine advertising company dedicated to helping lawyers and lawyer referral services get more clients through Google advertising. After seven years there as its president and CEO, he moved on to launch Matejka Marketing, Inc.

Ken has overseen the creation of numerous Google advertising and social media campaigns for law firms and bar associations, and over the years has directed the delivery of over 1.4 billion law-related ads in Google. As of this writing, Matejka Marketing provides marketing services to about 40 bar associations across the nation, as well as scores of law firms.

As a CLE presenter, Ken has given many seminars and webinars for bar associations across the country on the topics of website lead-generation for lawyers and related ethical issues.

Ken grew up in Rockford, Illinois and graduated from Marquette University in Milwaukee, Wisconsin in 1985. Since relocating to San Francisco, he has attended University of California, Hastings College of the Law, and the Masters in Taxation program at New York University.

Introduction

When it comes to getting more clients to make contact with your law firm, the current legal marketplace presents lawyers with significant challenges and amazing opportunities.

There are 37,000 people graduating from law school each year. These new lawyers compete with more established and experienced law firms, as well as with major legal directories, for a shrinking pool of clients, as many legal consumers choose self-help websites like LegalZoom or inexpensive legal advice websites like RocketLawyer.

Yet the Internet brings unprecedented opportunities as new marketing channels become available. This allows small law firms to compete for cases along with the well-funded marketing campaigns of the largest law firms and legal directories in their communities—at least for short bursts of time.

Figure 1. The shrinking San Francisco Yellow Pages, 2010 (bottom) through 2013 (top).

Gone are the days when a lawyer bought a Yellow Page "Double Truck" for a 12-month span and hoped for the best. The figure above shows that advertisers have been abandoning the Yellow Pages as an advertising vehicle due to its diminishing return on investment.

In the same way, in August 2015 Viacom reported that its television advertising revenue for the previous quarter was down 9%. As illustrated in the following figure, a massive sell-off of television media stock caused the major news media companies to lose $65 billion in market value in just 2 days. I see this as a clear sign that investors had no confidence in the future of television advertising.

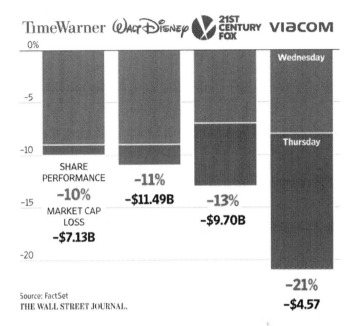

Figure 2. August 2015 market capitalization losses in the four major television news media companies.

In lieu of print and television advertising, Google, Bing, Yahoo, YouTube and other digital media give a lawyer unprecedented flexibility to reach the right audience when the consumer is actually in the mind set to hire a lawyer. Through digital marketing, for the first time, you have the opportunity to display ads only when you need to and to suspend or change your marketing message as the whim or need strikes.

The time is now to make this a great year for your law practice. You may be better than your competitors, but online success hinges primarily on visibility.

This book is intended to help the solo practitioner and small law firm attract as many legal consumers as possible into their law practice through what I call your "Online Leads Ecosystem." The book attempts to present a comprehensive look at what the Internet looks like for lawyers, what works for lead generation and what doesn't, and what a lawyer can do in-house to get more clients into his or her law practice.

While it is primarily intended for lawyers who represent individuals and small businesses, a lot of what is covered here applies equally to lawyers who represent medium-sized businesses. However, if your law practice is oriented towards insurance defense or major mergers and acquisitions, there is probably very little in this book that will help you generate the kinds of leads you're looking for.

As I discuss later in this book, the effectiveness of your website as a lead generator depends fundamentally on two factors: (1) how many visitors can be brought to your website and (2) how effective your website is in getting its visitors to make contact with your law firm.

This book addresses the first factor by showing how to amass a large number of visitors to your website. I also go into detail about elements of a successful law firm website, including the role of other online elements like social media that support your website.

Lead generation is important, but if you don't turn those leads into clients, it won't help with the growth of your law practice. Consequently, I spend a few pages discussing how closing a deal is different now than it may have been was 20 years ago when it was harder for consumers to contact lawyers and when there was no such thing as a legal directory outside of the Yellow Pages.

Finally I will address some of the ethical issues relating to your online content.

Much of the material in this book describes the various elements of your lead-generating online presence and offers an explanation of what each particular online marketing medium is used for and why it's important. I make frequent reference to your "Online Leads Ecosystem" which I will explain more fully throughout this book.

When I make reference to a specific service or product, like ApexChat for chat services or Squarespace for do-it-yourself website construction, it's not because I have any economic interest or affiliation with the company. I mention them only because I have found them a good value for what they deliver. This book isn't intended to be an exhaustive survey of every service that is available for lawyers and there are likely many good alternatives to the various companies I'm recommending throughout this book.

In a chapter towards the end of the book, there is a step-by-step guide to direct you towards the development of the optimal online lead-generating machine, and you are encouraged to skip right to that chapter at anytime, using the rest of the book for reference.

It may be evident as you read that no solo practitioner would have the time, energy or staff resources to do everything I write about in this book. After all, you probably prefer practicing law to posting to social media. Cognizant of the possible limitations on the typical solo practitioner's resources, the step-by-step guide focuses on only the essentials for creating the best possible lead generating ecosystem.

The material in this book is supported by nearly 30 years of data that I have gathered through my marketing efforts as Operations Manager of the Bar Association of San Francisco Lawyer Referral and Information Service. Since 2006, I have had the opportunity to display over 1.4 billion ads to people actively searching for legal help in Google.

My company, Matejka Marketing, Inc., provides comprehensive online marketing services for solo practitioners and small law firms and can help execute a marketing campaign for even the most modest of advertising budgets. Our services to law firms include custom websites, Google advertising, search engine optimization, social media management and everything else you read about in this book.

If you have any questions about the contents of this book or if you would like to talk with us about whether our marketing services are a good fit for your law practice, please call us or write to us:

Phone: (415) 513-8736

Email: info@matejkamarketing.com.

Chapter 1. A Quick Look at Google

Any book about online lead generation for lawyers must begin with recognition that an overwhelming majority of law-related searches in the United States begins in a Google search box.

A study reported in December 2015[1], analyst Eli Schwartz surveyed a large number of search engine users to determine which of the search engines were most preferred. For searches on desktop computers, Google's market share among those surveyed was 75%.

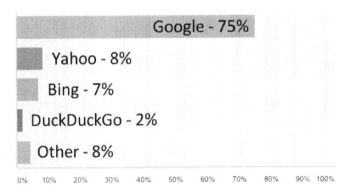

Figure 3. Search engine desktop usage preferences.

In the figure below, we see that user preference for Google on mobile devices is even more dominant than on desktop computers.

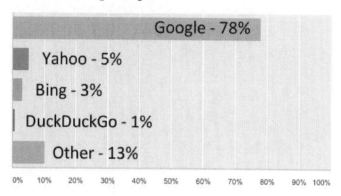

Figure 4. Search engine mobile usage preferences.

My considerable data over the last 10 years shows that Google's market share for law-related search is greater than the figures above indicate.

With Google's hundreds of millions of law-related searches each month (eclipsing Bing and Yahoo), being visible on the web for a lawyer means being visible in Google. Your website traffic data should show that the largest source of your website's traffic is coming from Google. If this is not the case, then your website is not visible enough.

When it comes to reaching people who are seeking legal help online, Google is the only show in town. As such, we must embrace it to get as much law-related traffic to your website as we can.

Throughout this book, I make reference to Google's "Sponsored Listings" and other times to Google's "organic" results. Here is an explanation of the two.

Google's Sponsored Listings

The "Sponsored Listings" are short text advertisements of a fixed number of characters that Google displays as part of its search results. The advertiser tells Google that it is willing to pay them a certain amount of money (the advertiser's "bid") if a Google user types in a search that the advertiser is bidding on (for example, an advertiser might bid on "personal injury lawyer" so that their ad shows when someone performs that search). If the Google user clicks on the ad, then the advertiser owes Google a sum of money based on their bid for the phrase (and a few other factors).

In the following figure, the Sponsored Listings ads are highlighted for a typical legal search result. Each of the advertisers listed in the Sponsored Listings in this figure have told Google that they are willing to pay Google up to a certain amount of money each time someone clicks on one of the ads.

Figure 5. "Sponsored Listings" highlighted.

You'll notice in the figure above that Google no longer displays ads in the right sidebar of its search results as it had for many years until last year. Additionally, rather than showing only three ads at the top of the page, it usually now shows four, putting pressure on advertisers to bid aggressively to show up in the top four positions. The fourth ad also has the

14

effect of pushing the organic results lower in the search results.

There's more discussion on the topic of Google's Sponsored Listings later in this book.

Google's Organic Results

The lower part of Google's search results are known as its "organic" results and consists of two parts. The process of getting your website visible in either (and hopefully both) of these parts of Google's search results is the point of what has come to be known as search engine optimization, which we discuss more fully later in this book.

The first part, shown below, is the maps results. It usually displays three results and is Google's best guess as to what is geographically closest to what the Google user is searching for.

The area where the map results appear is highlighted in the next figure.

Figure 6. Google's "Maps" results highlighted.

The second part of Google's organic results are drawn from Google's index. As with the maps, they are not paid results. Instead they are Google's ranking of websites that it has determined contain the most relevant content relating to the user's search. How your website ranks is for the most part mathematically based through Google's algorithm which is reported to consider over 200 factors in the determination of where a website is going to rank on a particular search. There is also often a manual component because Google has thousands of editors performing searches to ensure that the most important result is always in the first position. For example, if someone searches for the "Johnson & Smith Law Offices," Google wants to ensure as much as possible that the Johnson & Smith Law Offices website is in the first spot.

Figure 7. Google's index results highlighted.

While the maps results are supposed to be independent of the organic results, and the methods for getting your law firm in the two locations are different, there is a noticeable correlation between law firms that rank on the first page of Google's search results and those which show in the maps results.

Google vs. Bing/Yahoo

The following figure is a segment of a Google Analytics report from a high-volume, Midwestern legal service website for one month in 2014. It must be noted that this website is for the most part equally visible in the organic search results of all 3 search engines for the same search terms.

In this chart, "google/cpc" refers to the legal service provider's Google advertising in the "Sponsored Listing," and "google/organic" refers to visitors to this website through Google's organic results.

This Analytics snapshot is included here to show Google's enormous market share for law-related search in the United States. As the figure shows, for this particular website, Google's Sponsored Listings (paid advertising) and Google's organic results (Google's index) account for about 59.4% of the legal website's overall traffic.

While 59.4% may sound like a lot, it doesn't sound overwhelming. However, let's take away some of the data and compare only the organic traffic from the 3 search engines.

We first remove the "(direct)/(none)" traffic showing at 19.4%. Direct/none traffic refers to when someone arrives at a site by directly typing its URL or when Google doesn't know where they came from. For this particular legal services provider, the majority of this direct traffic was likely from the firm's staff.

Source / Medium ⑦	Acquisition	
	Sessions ⑦ ↓	
	3,794	
	% of Total: 100.00% (3,794)	
1. google / cpc	**1,589** (41.88%)	
2. ▓▓▓▓▓▓▓▓▓▓▓▓	**736** (19.40%)	
3. google / organic	**456** (12.02%)	
4. (direct) / (none)	**239** (6.30%)	
5. semalt.semalt.com / referral	**205** (5.40%)	
6. yahoo / organic	**45** (1.19%)	
7. bing / organic	**38** (1.00%)	
8. smallclaims.fcmcclerk.com / referral	**21** (0.55%)	
9. m.facebook.com / referral	**19** (0.50%)	
10. youtube-downloader.savetubevideo.com / referral	**19** (0.50%)	

Figure 8. Traffic sources for a high-volume, Midwestern legal website.

Now we have 456 visitors from Google's organic results and 83 from Bing/Yahoo. We can see that Google's share of the search engine traffic is 84.6% with Yahoo[2] at 8.3% and Bing at 7%.

This is typical of the scores of law firms' Analytics reports to which I have access. Data like this helps us focus on what's most important when we're helping small law firms and solo practitioners have limited resources to invest in online visibility.

Our takeaway here is this: if you have first page visibility in Google for certain searches, you'll probably be reaching about 85% of the people performing those searches. If you have first page visibility in Bing for the same searches, you'll be reaching about 7% of the people performing those searches. If we want volume, and we do, we need Google visibility.

Google vs. Personal Referrals

Someone who needs a lawyer is going to first ask a friend or relative for a personal referral, right?

Historically, the answer to this question was "yes, of course." Not anymore.

As the Operations Manager of the Lawyer Referral & Information Service (LRIS) of the Bar Association of San Francisco, I had the opportunity to examine referral source data dating back to 1983, which was the year our LRIS got its first digital database. From 1983 until about 2005, the top three referral sources were as follows, often in this order:

- Friend, relative, or colleague

- Other attorney

- Yellow Pages

Around 2005, Google replaced the Yellow Pages as the number 3 referral source, and since 2013, for the first time since 1983 ,"Friend, relative, or colleague" and "Other attorney" have been displaced from the first and second positions, with Google being by far the top referral source.

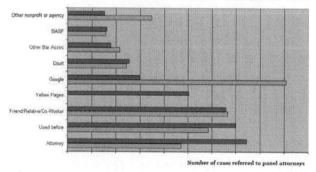

Bar Association of San Francisco LRIS Top Referral Sources

Number of cases referred to panel attorneys

Figure 9. Bar Association of San Francisco top referral sources (2013).

This is a significant development that speaks to the changing habits of online consumers, which we discuss more later in this book.

Note in the figure above that this is not merely the number of consumers who contacted the program – this chart shows the number of actual referrals, showing Google as the most productive source of good cases.

Also notice the significant decline since 2005 in "Other Attorney" as a referral source. I see this as possibly a combination of two factors: First, many lawyers may be less discriminating than they used to be, taking cases that they might have passed on before. Second, consumers are growing more inclined to make the process of selecting an attorney more of a personal matter, with trusted online review sites like Yelp making it easier to find a good lawyer without involving friends in the process. We discuss this latter group in more detail in the next chapter.

22

Chapter 2. Knowing the Online Legal Consumer

Who Searches for a Lawyer Online?

If someone needs a lawyer, they have a lot of options available to help with their search. If they know a lawyer, they could get a personal referral. If they don't know a lawyer, but they know someone who knows a lawyer, then they might get a personal referral.

In the past, if either of the above scenarios were the case, then the consumer would seek out the personal referral. This is why your referral network of other attorneys has always been, and may always be your best source of clients.

The personal referral serves as a recommendation, making the consumer more comfortable contacting the lawyer who has been prescreened (maybe) by their friend or colleague, the referral source.

People without connections to the legal community

What if someone needs a lawyer, but has no connection to the legal community, nor do they know anyone who has? This is a larger group of legal consumers than one would think, especially for areas of law like personal injury.

Much of this group consists of lower- and middle-income people, trades-people, schoolteachers, and the like.

Many of these consumers can afford a lawyer and often have serious legal matters. Even the lowest income people of this group get injured in auto accidents or can raise enough money to pay attorneys' fees for a DUI that threatens their ability to drive a car.

People who prefer deciding for themselves

What about people who know lawyers but would rather not get a personal referral?

In this group are people who may not want to involve friends or relatives in the search for personal reasons. For example, if someone needs a divorce lawyer, they may not want to ask their father-in-law for a referral.

Regardless of how personal or embarrassing a person's legal issue may be, there is also a growing number of people who would rather do the research and choose a lawyer based on their own criteria. A recent survey found that 85% of consumers trust online reviews as much as a personal recommendation and that 49% of consumers need at least a four-star rating before they choose to use a business.[3]

This point is further supported by LRIS referral source data showing Google's displacement of "Friend, relative, or colleague" and "Other attorney" as top referral sources (see Chapter 1 for more on this).

Businesses clients

There is a belief among some that Google visibility is important for law firms that represent individual consumers but that it won't generate leads for law firms targeting businesses with commercial legal issues.

The business attorney may find that their main referral source is their network of colleagues and that the Internet has not been a significant source of leads. One might conclude that the Internet, therefore, is not a good source for gaining commercial clients.

This is not the case. I manage Google advertising for successful business attorneys who get good clients from Google.

Mom-and-pop businesses would fall within one of the consumer categories above, but small to medium businesses will sometimes use Google. Among these business owners are those who would rather choose for themselves. Other instances may include company managers who are given the task by higher-ups to find counsel for some specific matter.

A third type of business case that may come as a result of a Google search would be a law firm somewhere else that needs local counsel in your jurisdiction and simply doesn't have a referral source.

What Do Online Consumers Want to Know About You?

Your advertising and website must be tailored to meet the needs and expectations of the modern Internet user. Once your ideal client has arrived on your website, you need to tell them what they want to know about you.

People who have never had to hire a lawyer before sometimes are intimidated by lawyers and by the hiring process. It's important to keep in mind that your message should exude a certain friendliness and approachability, especially for areas like elder law and family law. This is also true for criminal defense, personal injury law and most other practice areas.

While your website should show you to be engaging and approachable, your message should speak to the desires of the specific user. For example, someone who needs a criminal defense lawyer may be drawn to the message that you are "tough as nails," and if you are a personal injury lawyer, they may respond best to "millions recovered for our clients." An elder law attorney should convey the message that he or she is caring and compassionate.

It's been found that many online consumers are less concerned about where you went to law school or how long you've been practicing law than they are about why you became a lawyer and what you do in service to the community. In one 2015 study, it was found that 87% of consumers say they would move from one brand to another if that brand was associated with a good cause.[4] This is referred to by some as "cause marketing."

My company, Matejka Marketing, Inc., supports the work of a charity oriented towards helping people in Kenya get access to clean drinking water. Saying it prominently on your website helps with your "cause marketing." If you have anything philanthropic associated with your law practice, certainly say it on your website. The additional exposure may heighten awareness of the cause and make a good impression on your visitors.

THANKS TO OUR CLIENTS

Matejka Marketing proudly supports the mission of Just One Africa to bring water filtration devices to families in Kenya. Visit *Just One Africa* to learn how you can help too.

Figure 10. Example of conspicuous "cause marketing."

That being said, if your philanthropic activity is religious or political in nature, consider the impact the impression it may make on some of your desired client-types.

If you don't have anything that would fit within the category of cause marketing, consider donating a small monthly sum of money to your local food bank or something like that. Then boast about it.

How Long Will They Wait for Your Response?

Most legal services are sold in a "thin market" and as such, people who need to hire a lawyer are likely to make their decision fairly quickly (with a few notable practice-area exceptions like estate planning and adoption). There is more on this topic in the following chapter.

It has been found that people grow very impatient when waiting for a response from an online inquiry – an "intent-rich micro-moment," as Google dubs it. The Internet makes it easy for someone to make contact with more than one law firm, thus it becomes a race.

And please answer the phone.

People may be more patient after hours, but during regular business hours, try to have a person, rather than a machine, answer your phone. Many people will abandon the call quickly if the phone is answered by a machine.

I had an opportunity to examine over 2,000 regular business hours phone calls to one of my high-volume clients, which had an answering machine answering every one of those phone calls before speaking with a person. Among these callers, I found that about 7% of them hung up by the 5th second and 15% hung up by the 10th second.

You invest a lot in terms of effort and money to get leads into your law practice and we must make the most of every inquiry.

Chapter 3. Legal Services as a Thin Market

What is a "Thin Market"?

A "thin market" is a term used to describe a marketplace where there are few consumers who are buying something that they need maybe only once or twice in their lifetimes about which they make the decision fairly quickly. A classic example is when someone's refrigerator breaks. That person perhaps has never been in a situation where they needed to buy a refrigerator before, but they need to do so today so that their food doesn't spoil. Considerations such as "Can it be delivered today?" and "Will it fit within the dimensions of my kitchen cabinets?" take precedence over cost and brand. And once the consumer decides upon the refrigerator, they are not back in the market for a refrigerator for perhaps another 20 years.

For most areas of law, legal services are like this.[5] Many consumers have never had to hire a lawyer before, yet find themselves at a crisis point where they feel that they must hire a lawyer as soon as possible to deal with the legal matter at hand. In this case, and millions of times a day, such people open a Google search box and start looking. After making contact with several law firms by phone or email, soon they will have had one or two good conversations and have one or more in-office consultations set up for the following next few days.

Reaching the Online Legal Consumers at the Micro-Moment That They Need You

When marketing to the modern online consumer, it is essential to get your message in front of them at the moment that he or she decides that it is time to hire a lawyer. Google says that the mobile revolution has eliminated the normal sales funnel for many services as consumers have grown to expect immediate fulfillment of their needs.

Google refers to this as the "Micro-moment:"

"Micro-moments occur when people reflexively turn to a device—increasingly a smartphone—to act on a need to learn something, do something, discover something, watch something, or buy something . . . In these moments, consumers' expectations are higher than ever. The powerful computers we carry in our pockets have trained us to expect brands to immediately deliver exactly what we are looking for when we are looking. We want things right, and we want things right away."

Advertising by local legal service providers has changed dramatically since the widespread adoption of the smartphone as the preferred device for accessing the Internet.

Yellow Pages print advertising is a fading memory of a bygone era. The Internet presents amazing opportunities to reach legal consumers, with a great deal of precision and, if we want, at a fraction of the cost of what we used to pay the Yellow Pages.

Advertising channels like Google, YouTube, Facebook and Twitter allow lawyers, in varying degrees, to target legal consumers by where they are geographically located, by interests, age and gender, by area of law, by day or week and time of day, by device type and more. And the breadth and depth of the data relating to how legal consumers search is incredible.

This section will describe a few of the key metrics to be aware of so you can refine and narrow your use of online advertising to make the most of your marketing budget.

When do people search for legal help?

It's been found generally that legal consumers, like all consumers, are task-oriented during the week, particularly in the mornings, and that by late afternoon and weekends, their searches tend to be more entertainment and news-related. In the chart below, we see e-mail inquiries by time of day for a high-volume legal website for a period of four months in 2015.

You'll see that people are most likely to make contact with the legal service provider between 10 AM and 2 PM. For advertising, we'll want to make sure our ads (whether it's Google or any other online advertising channel) are scheduled to run at least for those hours of the day. For staffing, we want to try as much as possible to have maximum coverage by phone, email, text and chat during those hours.

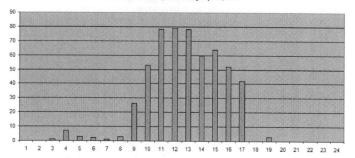

Figure 11. Inquiries by time of day.

In the following chart, we see inquiries to the same legal website by day of week, extending back through the nine years that I have been managing their Google advertising. Overall, you'll see that Tuesdays are the most productive days, with Mondays close behind.

As with time of day, with a small advertising budget, we want our ads to be running as much as possible on Tuesdays. Then, if we have the budget, on Mondays. Then Thursdays, Wednesdays and finally Fridays. Likewise, we should keep these high-volume periods of time in mind when scheduling our intake staff.

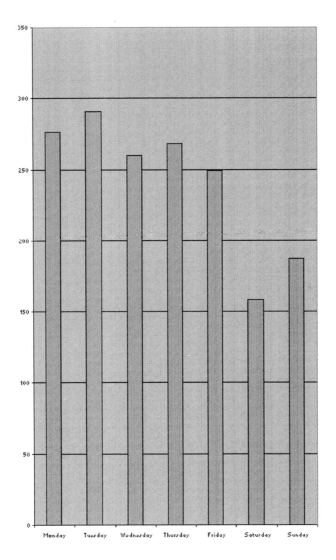

Figure 12. Inquiries by day of week.

What phrases are they searching for?

It is probably obvious that the highest volume law-related searches are very general in nature. The highest volume search terms shown in the chart below are the single words "lawyer," "lawyers," "attorney," and "attorneys," accounting for 35% of all searches. Variations of "legal aid" weighed in at 6%. Out of 2,401 search terms that we're currently bidding on in this particular English-language Google campaign, the top 30 search phrases (each search phrase including variations of "lawyer" and "attorney") account for 71% of the overall search volume.

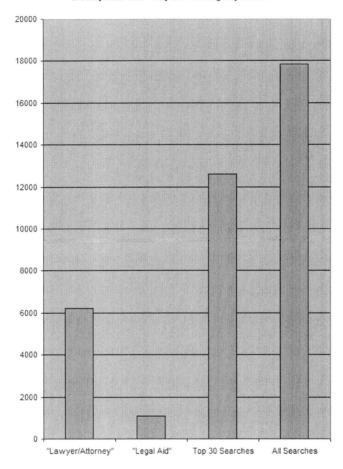

Search Terms - Relative Volume
Brooklyn Bar LRS - May 2014 through April 2015

Figure 13. Highest-volume search terms.

Naturally, the highest volume search phrases happen to be the most competitive, and most expensive, to target. In a self-managed campaign, a large volume of local legal consumers can be reached by bidding upon just a few dozen phrases, but by bidding on the other several thousand less competitive phrases, you stretch your marketing dollar the furthest. Consequently, you should make an effort to build out your search phrase inventory as much as you can.

What devices are they using?

The chart below shows inquiries in 2014 to the Bar Association of San Francisco Lawyer Referral & Information Service (LRIS) by the type of device the legal consumer was using to make contact with the program. As you'll see, the device used most often to make contact with the lawyer referral service in English and Spanish was a smartphone.

Not surprisingly, when an LRIS does not have a mobile-formatted version of its website, the smartphone is found not to be a significant source of inquiries. This causes the legal service provider to miss out on a significant percentage of inquiries that it could be receiving.

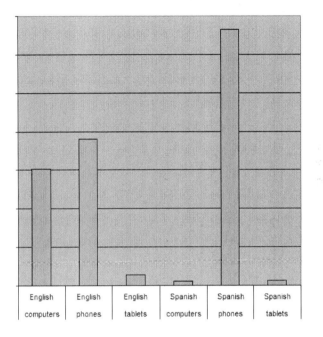

Figure 14. Inquiries by device type.

It is worth noting that if a legal consumer is searching in Google in the Spanish language and makes contact with an advertiser, our data shows that almost always the user makes contact by click-to-call through a smartphone. This is virtually to the exclusion of all other device types, as shown in the chart above.

Finally, it is further worth noting that Google has a near monopoly of the smartphone search market, being the default search engine on Androids and iPhones.

It is recommended that your marketing budget, if it is less than unlimited, be weighted towards advertising to people who are searching on smartphones, allocating less of your budget towards desktop advertising.

While my findings above relate to the advertising of bar associations, my data is consistent for law firms in our portfolio as well. Legal consumer search behavior is the same regardless of the type of legal services provider.

Branding in a Thin Market

Branding is one of those concepts that can be very valuable in certain industries but an inefficient use of marketing resources in thin markets where brand considerations are secondary to other more immediate concerns.

For example, in the soft drink market (which is *not* a thin market), branding is important because all colas are basically the same. Through relentless and costly branding efforts, Coca-Cola convinces consumers that drinking their cola is better than drinking that of other brands. Their message is not that their soft drinks taste better but that it is better to associate with their brand. While Coca-Cola is famous for how successful it is in its branding efforts, it has come at an extreme cost that very few companies can afford.

Yet, when consumers are seldom in the marketplace for your service and they tend to decide fairly quickly, it's much more important to deliver your message exactly in the intent-rich micro-moment when they need you, rather than spending limited marketing resources trying to drive your law firm's name into their minds should they at some future time need you.

Does branding work for legal services?

No one will deny that it's important for people to view your business as superior to other companies providing similar services. Through branding efforts, we attempt to convince consumers that our law firm is the best among many in our practice area(s). The idea is basically, when they need legal services, they will remember you and call you because you're the best.

For law firm branding, the problem is with the "remembering when they need you" part.

For legal services, I don't believe it works well enough to warrant any significant marketing investment.

As proof, ask any non-lawyer to name three personal injury law firms in your community. Really, do this and see what you find. I'd wager that non-lawyers you ask will not be able to do so despite the tens of thousands of dollars spent each month in your community on personal injury billboards, bus placards, and newspaper ads.

I ask this question at my Continuing Legal Education seminars and often only the personal injury lawyers in attendance can name three local personal injury law firms. Even other lawyers in attendance struggle to come up with three.

Why is that?

For a brand to be memorable, the consumer needs to think about the product or service after they view or hear the message in the advertisement. However, a person naturally avoids thinking about unpleasant things.

It is unpleasant to have a legal problem and face the prospect of hiring a lawyer and incurring legal fees. Do people want to think about how they may someday be seriously injured in an auto accident? No, they do not and I believe that a consumer is likely to drive that thought out of their heads. And without the thoughtful reflection about the message and about the company delivering it, nothing is remembered.

If you passed three billboards or saw three print ads, which message is likely to conjure the most reflection?

- Non-stop flights to Maui,

- The newest, greatest iPhone, or

- A law firm for when you're injured in an auto accident.

People may disagree, but I personally would think most about the Maui flight. I suggest that the first two messages are likely to take up much more neural bandwidth in most (or all) consumers than thoughts about getting mangled in a painful, traumatic car crash, or getting arrested for DUI.

Imagine how much thought a consumer would give to an ad for a crematorium or cancer treatment facility? Not very much. Law firm branding for a lot of practice areas can be like that.

This is not to say that branding is without value. If there is a general perception in the marketplace that your law firm is better than any other law firm and if your listing is among many in Google's search results, the consumer may choose your law firm first. I just think it's not an optimal use of a law firm's marketing investment.

Assuming your law firm has less than an unlimited amount of money to invest in marketing, your resources would be much more productive in direct marketing, getting your message in front of consumers while they are actively searching for legal help.

Chapter 4. Your Online Leads Ecosystem

What Is Your "Online Leads Ecosystem"?

"Online Leads Ecosystem" is a term used in this book to describe the online infrastructure and processes you have in place to get clients into your law practice. Your Ecosystem is the growing build-out of your online content and activities and includes your website, social media, YouTube, blog, podcasts, and anything else you may do online to boost your visibility among people who may need your help.

It's helpful to compare your online activity to what you have been doing off of the web for what may be many years and how it translates to your Online Leads Ecosystem.

The following figure shows what you probably do currently to get more clients to contact your firm, all of which is completely unrelated to the Internet.

For this comparison, let's call it your "Analog Leads Ecosystem." As you see, your Analog Leads Ecosystem is an assortment of activities that you use to get your name into the community. At the core of your Analog Ecosystem would be your telephone number and business card.

Figure 15. Components of your Analog Leads Ecosystem.

To compare, the following figure shows the digital equivalents of your analog activities. It is worth noting at this point that while you are developing your Online Leads Ecosystem, your Analog Leads Ecosystem will continue to be important to your law firm's business development, with the exception of your analog advertising which is of diminishing importance, if not obsolete.

Figure 16. Components of your Online Leads Ecosystem.

How Your Online Leads Ecosystem Helps Your Law Practice

Your optimal Online Leads Ecosystem (hereinafter, your "Ecosystem") will bring traffic to one or more of your online properties, whether it's your website, YouTube channel, Facebook Fan Page, or something else.

Usually people looking for legal help will begin their search at Google, but occasionally they may go to Yelp, Bing, Yahoo or some other resource. Their point of entry into your Ecosystem will usually depend on which of your pages or platforms appears to Google to be most relevant to Google (or Yahoo/Bing). This may be your YouTube channel, your Facebook Fan Page, one of your blog posts, etc.

In February 2015, Google entered into a deal with Twitter that gives Google full access to index Twitter in real time. This makes Twitter an important entry point into your ecosystem – again through a Google search.

Your optimal Ecosystem will be visually inviting and rich in emotive, readable (and just as importantly, skimmable) content. This content needs to always be formatted properly for the device that the legal consumer uses to access your information, whether it is a smartphone, Kindle, iPad or PC, the most important of which is the smartphone.

Your appealing and properly formatted content will cause people who come into your Ecosystem to stay there and ultimately in varying percentages to make contact with you. When the visitor is from your advertising, the contact rate ideally should be at least 15% of the time.

The platforms and pages of your Ecosystem will conspicuously invite people to make contact with you by phone, live chat, email, text or your contact form.

And the last critical step, your most important role in the optimal functioning of your Ecosystem, is to jump on that inquiry and close that deal.

In brief, here's what you get from a well-developed Online Leads Ecosystem:

1. Lots of Traffic +

2. Great Web Presence = Leads.

3. You Close the Lead = Clients

Most of the remainder of this book will be a more detailed breakdown of each of these three elements, but briefly, they are as follows:

1. "Lots of Traffic" means that there are a good number of people actively searching for legal help in your practice areas and community, and that these people are visiting your website or one of your other online properties. What is a "good number" will vary geographically and by practice area, and the goal naturally is to get as much of this traffic into your ecosystem as possible.

2. "Great Web Presence" refers primarily to your website, and may include other well-developed web properties like Facebook, that cause people to make contact with you in acceptable numbers. A bad website will produce very little for you regardless of how much traffic you get to it, whereas an extraordinary website will produce a lot for you, even with less traffic.

3. "You Close the Lead" refers to the process that you have in place to get that potential client into your office. Many excellent lawyers are not the best salespeople, yet that's a very important part of the Ecosystem. Consequently, we're going to discuss a sales process in a later chapter.

How Much Traffic Do You Need to Get a Client?

Before we get into how to draw visitors into your Ecosystem, let's briefly discuss how many visitors you may actually need to successfully get a client in your caseload.

As a point of qualification, there will be instances where you will need less traffic to get clients. For example, if you are practicing in an obscure area of law or in a rural community where consumers have fewer choices, people may be more likely to make contact with you and you'll need less traffic to get the quantity of leads you want. Conversely, if you have a general practice in a large city, you may need more traffic, and it is this latter situation that is described here.

A final consideration is the quality of the traffic you are getting to your website. One hundred visitors from Google should result in more inquiries than 100 visitors from Facebook because people searching for legal help in Google are more likely to be in the "micro-moment" of the buying process.

For your website to be a lead generator, you need a lot of visitors and inquiries. The amount of traffic you need in order to get leads depends in large part on your website and you.

If your website appears dated, is underdeveloped, is not formatted for mobile devices, or contains content that reads like it was transcribed from a legal dictionary, it is possible that not many website visitors will be drawn to make contact with your law firm. A website like this will require a larger number of website visitors, possibly a much larger number, than would a more attractive, modern, optimally performing website.

Our data shows that a successful website should result in at least 15% of its visitors making contact with you. A very good website could have 20% of its visitors making contact with you. For purposes of this book, this is your website's "inquiry rate."

As an example of a legal website that performs extraordinarily well, consider the website of the Houston Lawyer Referral Service. For the first six months of 2015, the overall inquiry rate of this website was 21.51%, making it among the best performing legal website in our current portfolio. It is worth noting that a lawyer referral website and a law firm website are not substantially different in their target audiences, marketing methods and overall performance. The services that a lawyer referral service offer differ from a law firm that provides direct legal services but from the perspective of the consumer, it is akin to a directory or joint advertising for solo practitioners.

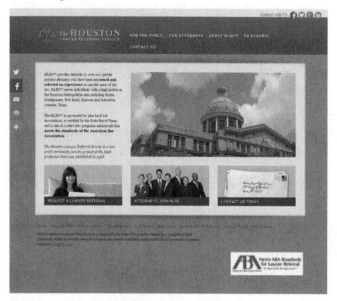

Figure 17. Houston LRS homepage (www.hlrs.org).

The smartphone version of the Houston LRS website has an astonishing 31.79% inquiry rate and calls through this mobile website account for almost 85% of all inquiries through their Google advertising in the first six months of 2015.

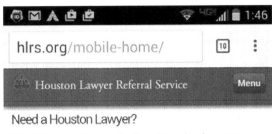

Figure 18. Houston LRS mobile-formatted website.[6]

To show how important inquiry rate is, imagine that there are 1,000 visitors to your website over some period of time, maybe a few weeks, maybe a few months. If your website causes 1% of your website visitors to make contact with you, then mathematically, that is 10 inquiries. If 5% of your website visitors contact you, that's 50 inquiries. If 10%, then you'd get 100 inquiries. Naturally, 100 inquiries will yield more good leads than 10 inquiries, and this is why a great website is so important.

Some of these inquiries will be of value, but we all know that not all of these inquiries are going to be good cases. No one needs to practice law for long before the lawyer realizes that a lot of the calls and emails they receive are not very good. Some people can't afford to hire an attorney, their statute of limitations lapsed years ago, their legal matter is in another state, they're not of sound mind, or some combination of the above.

But let's say that one out of five of those inquiries is something of interest. If so, then you will have received two possible leads from the website with the 1% inquiry rate as compared to 20 possible leads from the website with the 10% inquiry rate. The 18 extra inquiries will have a significant positive impact on your bottom line.

Once your website gets its website visitors to make contact with you, your job is to convert them to clients.

Using a 10% inquiry rate as our baseline, if you have 300 visitors to your website, you should receive 30 inquiries, and if your website converts at 15%, then you should receive 45 inquiries:

300 visitors ==> 30 to 45 inquiries

Of the 30 to 45 inquiries, we discussed earlier that most of these inquiries probably won't be legal matters that you would consider and maybe only one out of five may contain a legal issue of interest to you.

If one out of five of the inquiries is of interest, then there should be maybe between six and nine viable legal matters within that set of 30 to 45 inquiries.

300 visitors ==> 30 to 45 inquiries ==> 6 to 9 viable legal matters

These six to nine leads are the people in the micro-moment of the hiring process to whom you must IMMEDIATELY RESPOND. If you respond quickly and are a good closer, it is expected that you will get maybe one or two of these six leads, possibly three, and maybe (but not likely) most of them into your office for a longer conversation, steering towards the establishment of an attorney-client relationship.

Fortunately, of the four components of this equation, three parts are under your control:

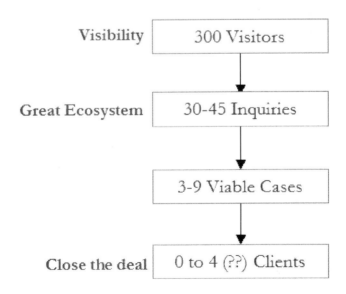

Visibility	300 Visitors
Great Ecosystem	30-45 Inquiries
	3-9 Viable Cases
Close the deal	0 to 4 (??) Clients

Figure 19. Approximate volume of visitors needed to get clients.

I. The more visible you are, the faster that 300 people with legal issues will be coming to your website.

II. The number of inquiries from those 300 visitors will depend upon how attractive people find your website, which includes development of engaging content, selection of attractive stock photography, and the creation of a version of your website for mobile devices.

III. The quality of the cases and the percentage of which might be of interest to you are not matters you can control because people with good cases and people with bad cases will find you using the same search terms.

IV. Finally, the number of inquiries that you convert to clients is entirely on you. This will depend on the immediacy of your response to the consumer's inquiry, your apparent empathy towards their plight, your expertise in their legal issue, and your subsequent sales process for getting as many people as possible into your office.

Chapter 5. Evaluating the Current State of Your Ecosystem

Figuring Out What Is Already in Place and Working

If you've been practicing for a while, chances are you have a website and some of your Online Leads Ecosystem is already in place. We need to take a hard look at everything because we don't want to throw out an element that is already working well. You may have good or at least salvageable pieces in place, which will save you time, effort and money.

The rest of this chapter is on the topic of figuring out (1) what you have in place currently that's working, (2) what is built but needs work, and (3) where the critical gaps are that need to be filled. In this chapter, I will focus on the core of your Ecosystem, your law firm's website, and in later chapters, I will discuss other Ecosystem elements in more detail, such as your Yelp listing and Twitter account.

The previous chapter addressed the main parts of your Online Leads Ecosystem that are under your control, namely (1) the attractiveness and productivity of your website so that people who come to it choose to make contact with you, (2) the visibility of your website so that there are a lot of people accessing it, and (3) your ability to close the deal so that the people who reached out to you become paying clients.

Is there a breakdown?

If there's a breakdown somewhere, a weak link in your chain, there's a possibility that it is in only one place. For example, if you're a great closer and there's a lot of traffic on your website, then maybe you only need to focus on making the website more appealing to get more of the people who go there to make contact with you.

On the other hand, if the data shows very little traffic and you have trouble closing the few leads that you get, but the people who come to your website appear to respond well to it, then you may be able to put website work on the back burner and focus on your visibility and sales process.

Or maybe your website gets very little traffic, very few people make contact with you, and it's hard to close even those few. In this case, the breakdown is in several places. The good news is that it's completely fixable—we just have some work to do.

So let's go through these three parts—your website, your visibility, and your sales process—to see if there's a roadblock somewhere and what can be done to make your Online Leads Ecosystem perform optimally.

How Effective Is Your Current Website at Getting People to Make Contact with You?

How do we know if your website is doing its job?

There are several ways that we can get an answer to this. We have three good information sources to help us determine how effective your website is as a lead generator. These are (1) your anecdotal data, (2) Google Analytics, and (3) Google advertising data.

> **NOTE:** We are not talking right now about how good your website is at bringing in a lot of traffic. Right now we are only talking about how the existing traffic, whether it's a lot or not very much, is responding to your website.

What is the anecdotal information telling you about your website?

The answer to this question is partly your gut feeling and partly what people who contact you are telling you about their referral sources. How do you feel about your website's performance and what are people saying?

When you ask people how they found out about you, and hopefully you always do, how often do they say "website" or "Internet" or "Google?" Anytime someone makes any reference to finding you online, that is a vote in favor of your website. If you haven't been asking people how they found you, then please start asking and put it in a spreadsheet for future reference. Ask even the people you cannot help.

When someone emails you or contacts you through your website's contact form, then that naturally is a vote in favor of your website.

Compare the combined sum to your other referral sources and hopefully the various web, Google and other Internet sources will constitute your largest number of inquiries.

If you seldom receive emails or contact form submissions from your website and no one ever references your website when you're asking how they found out about you, there may be cause for concern. Absent any other reliable data, it may be time to start thinking about a website facelift or overhaul, as the case may be.

We should keep in mind, though, that even if no one ever references your website, the website may still be good. It could be that no one mentions your website because no one can find it. Evaluating the visibility of your website is a topic for later in this chapter.

In sum, when you find people referencing your website, the Internet, or Google frequently and you receive emails through it, and it's your largest referral source in the aggregate, then that's an indication that your website may be doing its job.

What is your Google Analytics data telling you about your website?

The second way we measure the effectiveness of your website is through Google Analytics. Analytics is a free data-gathering tool that Google makes available to anyone who wants it. The amount of data you can access through it is overwhelming and for purposes of this section, we're only going to talk about a small

part of your Analytics data that gives us a quick snapshot of how people are responding to your website.

> **IMPORTANT:** If you do not have Google Analytics in your website or if you are not sure whether you do, please talk to your website content manager and see to it that this is done as soon as possible. Without this data about your website visitors, you're missing out on a tremendous amount of very useful information about what is working and not working for your law practice. And it's free.

Analytics provides us a with wide variety of data gathered about your website's traffic, including how much traffic is coming in and where your traffic is coming from. For our purposes here, where using the Analytics data to see what it can tell us about how people are responding to your website generally.

Visitor behavior

When you have the Analytics code in your website, you log in to your dashboard to get general information about what your visitors are doing on your site once they get there. A deeper look into a lot of extremely useful data is beyond the scope of this book, but here are some of the key pieces of information that will help you roughly evaluate your web presence.

The figure below shows a portion of a typical Analytics dashboard. For each category of data displayed here, you can navigate to more specific information. For example, in the category "Users" (meaning visitors to your website), you can navigate down to which pages they viewed or which websites they came from to get to yours.

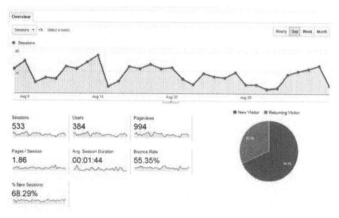

Figure 20. The Analytics dashboard.

What does this data tell us about how people are responding to your website?

The first piece of information to look at is your website's "Bounce Rate." A "bounce" is when someone visits your website and leaves the website without viewing a second page. That is to say, the visitor bounces out. "Bounce Rate" is the percentage of people who bounce out of your website as compared to all visitors.

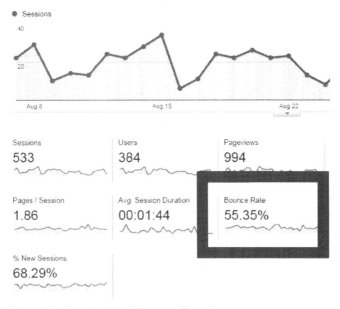

Figure 21. A website's "Bounce Rate."

Your website's bounce rate is important because it tells us how inviting people are finding your content. If your bounce rate is 80%, for example, then that is a clear indication that there are problems with your website. If your bounce rate is around 50%, then it suggests that people are being drawn into your website in adequate numbers. The lower your bounce rate, the better the website.

A high bounce rate is not decisive, however. If your traffic is low-quality or robotic, then your bounce rate may be artificially high. If the bulk of your traffic is coming to your blog, that will also cause an artificially high bounce rate because people learn from your blog posts what they need, then leave your website.

Google has said that it views a 75% bounce rate as acceptable, but I believe that is too high. The 55.35%

bounce rate for the website in the previous figure is reasonable but not great.

Other important metrics are pages per session and average session duration because they tell us how much of your content people are looking at and how much time they spend reading it. The more pages they view and the more time they spend on your website, the better.

The next figure shows where on your dashboard to find the information relating to pages per session (meaning how many pages your visitors viewed on average) and average session duration (meaning how much time on average people stayed on your website).

Figure 22. A website's pages per session and average session duration.

As with the bounce rate in the earlier figure, above, this website's numbers in these two areas are good, not great. If your pages per session are 1.2 and your average session duration is 45 seconds, that is an indication that people are not finding your content very interesting. As with bounce rate, these are general measures, not hard and fast data, because your numbers may be artificially low depending on the quality of your traffic.

Be sure that you're looking at the pages per session and average session duration of the most important pages of your website because your data could be distorted by other content categories on your website like your blog.

Percentage of people who view your "Thank You" page

If you have a page after your contact form that says something to the effect of "Thanks for your inquiry. We'll get back to you soon," then we can look at the traffic to that page to determine how often people successfully complete your contact form, which speaks to the effectiveness of your website in getting people to use the form to reach out to your law firm.

By comparing the number of people who come to your "contact us" page to the number of people who get to your "thank you" page, you'll get an idea of how moved website visitors are to use it.

You may not have a "Thank You" page or even a contact form for that matter, in which case this isn't going to work. If you are not sure whether you have a standalone "Thank You" page, simply send yourself a test submission through the form and check the name of the page in the address bar at the top of your browser. If the address of the page changes in your browser, then you probably have a "Thank You" page and all is good. If the address doesn't change, but instead is the same address as the contact form page, then the "thank you" message is probably dynamically generated and this useful Analytics data will not be obtainable.

To digress for a moment, traffic source data to your "Thank You" page will also help us determine which referral sources result in the most inquiries.

Analytics navigation changes often but as of this writing, to get to the content that visitors are viewing on your website, in the left hand margin, go here:

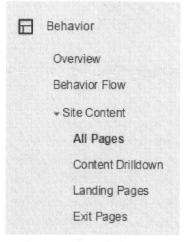

Figure 23. Analytics navigation to site content viewed by visitors.

Keep clicking through the pages until you find the thank you page. In the following figure, you'll see that it is in the 14th position.

Figure 24. Finding traffic data to your "Thank You" page in your Analytics account.

Once you have clicked on the page link itself, choose "Secondary dimension" and then "Source" to find where the traffic to your "Thank You" page is coming from, as shown in the next graphic.

65

Figure 25. Viewing the source of the traffic to your "Thank You" page.

The figure following is an example of what the data would look like.

Page		Source		Pageviews	
				183	
				% of Total: 0.56% (32,758)	
1. /contact/thank-you/		google		**116** (63.39%)	
2. /contact/thank-you/		(direct)		**38** (20.77%)	
3. /contact/thank-you/		BingYahoo		**9** (4.92%)	
4. /contact/thank-you/		yahoo		**8** (4.37%)	
5. /contact/thank-you/		bing		**5** (2.73%)	
6. /contact/thank-you/				**3** (1.64%)	
7. /contact/thank-you/		superlawyers.com		**2** (1.09%)	
8. /contact/thank-you/		comcast		**1** (0.55%)	
9. /contact/thank-you/		whatsupmag.com		**1** (0.55%)	

Figure 26. Traffic sources to "Thank You" page.

In the above graphic, we see the various channels that people use to reach this page. Notice that Google is by far the largest source of traffic to this page, accounting for approximately 63% of all contact form submissions for this 30-day period (remember that people can only view this page by successfully filling out your contact form).

This data is useful for determining which advertising channels are leading to visitors who use your contact form. This is very important because it tells you what advertising is working for you and what isn't. For example, if you are spending a lot of money on a directory listing but you are not seeing that directory website as a significant traffic source to your "Thank

You" page, your marketing dollars may be better spent elsewhere. Conversely, if you are spending very little on what appears to be a productive referral source, you may want to allocate more of your marketing dollars towards that resource.

Measuring website effectiveness using Google AdWords

The most reliable data comes from your Google advertising. If you have run ads in Google's Sponsored Listings and used "conversion tracking" in the course of your advertising, which we will cover in greater detail later, you will have very good information about how many people made contact with you after they came to your website through one of your ads.

"Call Details" tracking is another important metric to measure the usability of the smartphone version of your website (although call details metrics can be skewed by a poorly constructed or under-managed Google advertising account). We discuss phone call tracking a little later.

In Google advertising, the term "conversion" is used to describe a person making contact with you after clicking on one of your ads, usually through your contact form.[7] Earlier in this chapter, I talked about the "Thank You" page that people saw after they successfully filled out your contact form. With a "conversion tracking" script in that page, Google records the event. When someone clicks on one of your ads and finally arrives on your "Thank You" page, Google counts it as a conversion.

If you have conversion data, then we simply need to look at your "conversion rate," which is expressed in

AdWords as a percentage. A conversion rate of 10% means that 1 out of 10 people make contact with you through your contact form after clicking on one of your ads. Depending on how competitive your practice areas and community are (in terms of how many lawyers are advertising for the same client types), your conversion rate may be a little higher for niche areas (as an extreme example, let's say federal workers' compensation in a rural area) and lower for highly competitive areas (for example, car accidents in a large metropolitan area).

What is a good conversion rate?

Let's say your conversion rate is 3%. Regardless of your target practice areas or community, that is not very good. A conversion rate this low strongly points to a website that needs a facelift or overhaul. Conversely, if your conversion rate is 15% or better, this is a strong indication that your website is doing what it's supposed to be doing.

The next image shows data from a Google advertising account that my company manages for a law firm in a large metropolitan area. In this graphic, you will see that this law firm had 498 visitors ("clicks") for the time frame of this graph, and 98 of these visitors made contact with the law firm ("converted clicks").

In the last column Google does the math for us to show that this law firm's website causes over 19% of its visitors to make contact with the law firm. This is a terrific conversion rate, indicating concretely that people respond very strongly towards this law firm's website.

Campaign type	Clicks	Impr.	Converted clicks	Click conversion rate
Search Network only	498	13,103	98	19.84%

Figure 27. Google AdWords conversion rate.

If you have advertising data but are not conversion tracking, please pause your Google advertising and get the conversion tracking code into your website before you start running your ads again.

Phone call conversions

In the next figure, you see a table showing conversions (contact form inquiries) and phone calls, which is a count of the number of people who made contact with this legal website using their smartphones, usually by click-to-call, after performing a law-related search on their phone.

Campaign	Budget	Status	Conversions	Phone calls
Remarketing	$10.00/day	Limited by budget ?	11	0
Lawyers	Shared $42.00/day	Limited by budget ?	45	67
Spanish	$45.00/day	Eligible	27	34

Figure 28. Phone calls and contact form conversions, compared.

Notice here that for the "Lawyers"[8] and "Spanish" campaigns, mobile phone calls outnumber contact form inquiries. This information could tell us that this website has an easier-to-use mobile website that its desktop version, or it may indicate that in this community, people are more likely to make contact with the law firm on their smartphones that through a contact form.

A closer look at the data would give us a better sense of which of these scenarios is the case, but in any event, we can measure the strength or weakness of your mobile website by taking a look at how likely someone is to convert once arriving on the website by way of their smartphones.

The way you get to this information in your Google advertising dashboard is to select the campaign you want to examine, then choose the tab "Settings." Then choose "Devices" as shown in the next graphic.

Campaign: Lawyers

* Enabled   Type: Search Network only - All features Edit   Budget: Shared $42.00/day Edit
Active bid adjustments: Device

| Ad groups | Settings | Ads | Keywords | Audiences | Ad extensions | Dimensions | ▾ |

| All settings | Locations | Ad schedule | Devices |

Filter ▾   Segment ▾   Columns ▾   ☑   ⬇   View Change History

	Device	Bid adj. ?	Converted ↓ clicks ?	Click conversion rate ?	Avg. CPC ?	Cost / converted click ?
☐	Mobile devices with full browsers	+50%	29	32.58%	$4.70	$14.21
☐	Computers		12	5.13%	$3.58	$69.88
☐	Tablets with full browsers		0	0.00%	$3.24	$0.00
	Total		41	12.09%	$3.86	$31.77

Figure 29. Smartphone conversion rate.

You'll see in this figure that the smartphone version of this website is very successful at getting people to make contact with the advertiser - 32.58% for the first

70

6 months of 2015. Compare it to the poor conversion rate of the desktop version of this website - 5.13% (as an aside, the +50% bid adjustment in the chart above tells Google that we want to be much more aggressive on smartphones in our bidding due to the significant performance disparity between the phone and desktop versions of the website).

To summarize this section on website effectiveness, if the referral source information you get verbally from clients is often Internet-related and if your Analytics and AdWords data are showing a lot of traffic to your "Thank You" page, then your website may be good and perhaps no work needs to be done to it at this time (outside of possible changes to increase visibility which we cover later).

If no one ever references your website and if there is no traffic at all to your "Thank You" page, this is bad and your website may be in trouble (unless the problem is with the contact form itself - too many required fields can have a negative impact on the percentage of people who fill it out).

If you haven't been asking people how they found out about you, you don't have Analytics installed, you've never run Google advertising, and/or you don't have a "Thank You" page, then we have an extreme shortfall of information. If this is the case, contact me and we will try to figure out together what can be gleaned from the little information we have to work with.

Later in this book we look through the elements of what makes a website successful to see if you have all of the pieces in place.

Now we're familiar with a few useful tools to determine how inviting your website is. The next section discusses how to evaluate your website's overall visibility.

How Much Traffic Is Coming to Your Website Currently?

It's time to go back to our Analytics data, this time to see how many people are coming to your website and how they are getting there. This will be the measure of our visibility, or lack thereof.

By looking at "Users" in the next figure, you can see how many visitors have come to your website over the course of a selected period of time. A very low number of users would indicate that your website is not very visible.[9] As your visibility increases, the number of your visitors will increase.

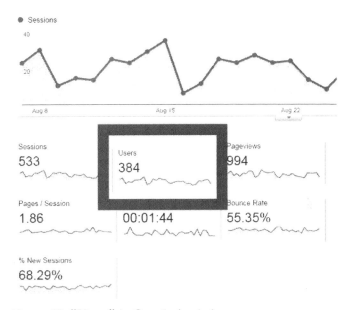

Sessions
40
20

Aug 8   Aug 15   Aug 22

Sessions	Users	Pageviews
533	384	994

Pages / Session		Bounce Rate
1.86	00:01:44	55.35%

% New Sessions
68.29%

Figure 30. "Users" in Google Analytics.

Where is your traffic coming from?

While not viewable from your default Dashboard, a very important piece of information is where your traffic is coming from. By navigating to "Acquisition/All Traffic," you can view traffic sources to give you an idea of how people are finding your website.

If your website is visible enough in the search engines, most of your website traffic should be coming from organic search, as shown in the next figure

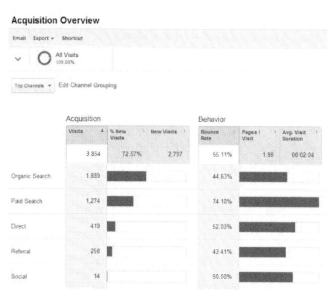

Figure 31. Organic traffic compared to all traffic types.

Since Google has an overwhelmingly large share of the law-related search market, it makes sense that you want most of your organic traffic to be coming from Google. If Google is not your most productive traffic source, then it is safe to conclude that your website is not visible enough in Google.

In the next figure, we see how to navigate to the traffic sources of your website to identify which websites are responsible for your website's traffic.

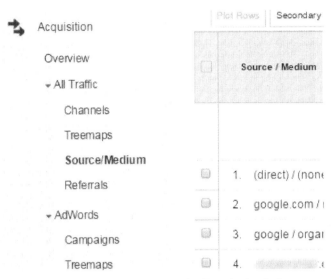

Figure 32. Viewing traffic sources in Google Analytics.

Source / Medium	Sessions
	1,520 % of Total: 100.00% (1,520)
1. google / organic	**749** (49.28%)
2. (direct) / (none)	**287** (18.88%)
3. google / cpc	**132** (8.68%)
4. ░░░░ .gov / referral	**65** (4.28%)
5. yahoo / organic	**43** (2.83%)
6. bing / organic	**36** (2.37%)
7. ░░░░ .org / referral	**29** (1.91%)
8. ░░░░ .org / referral	**25** (1.64%)
9. ░░░░ .org / referral	**19** (1.25%)
10. google.com / referral	**13** (0.86%)

Figure 33. Google traffic compared to all traffic sources.

In the figure above and the figure following, from the same Analytics data set, you'll see that about half of this website's traffic comes from Google organic.

If your Analytics data is showing that Google is not your biggest traffic source, we need to work towards increasing your visibility there.

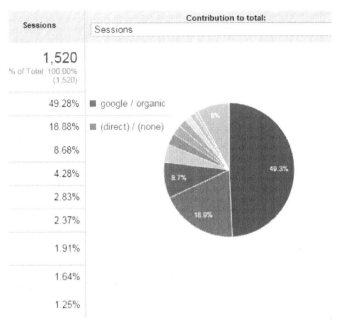

Figure 34. Pie-chart view of top referral sources.

Now we have an overview of how to evaluate how well your website and visibility efforts are working. Later in this book, we'll go through the actual evaluation process step-by-step.

How Quickly Can You Respond to Inquiries?

So now we have a sense of how to determine how long it takes us to get those hypothetical 300 visitors to our website and what percentage of them choose to make contact with you once they get there. The last part of the equation relates to how effective you are at closing the deal. If you receive six viable inquiries from 300 visitors to your website, how many of those leads can you get into your office and close? This topic we reserve for a later chapter.

Chapter 6. Entry Points, Points of Engagement, and Supporting Elements

Your website is foundational to everything you do online to get leads into your law practice. And everything you do related to your Online Leads Ecosystem will be towards the support of your website as a lead generator.

Most of the rest of this book is spent describing the development of your optimal Ecosystem with your website at its core. But before we get into that, we need to discuss the three categories into which all of our Ecosystem elements fall: entry points, points of engagement, and supporting elements.[10]

The reason it's important to understand each of these categories is that it will help us understand the role each of our online activities has in supporting your lead generator, i.e., your website. The relative importance of these various roles will help us assess the state of our Ecosystem's development and prioritize our Ecosystem development efforts in light of our less than unlimited resources.

Entry Points

An entry point in your Ecosystem refers to a direct path from one online location to your website. That is to say, it is a point from which a person will enter your website. The clearest example of an entry point would be your Google advertising where people enter your website by clicking on your ad. Other examples of entry points may be your social media, where people are clicking on a link on your Facebook Fan Page and entering your website.

To illustrate, in the graphic below, each of the channels shown here can be entry points to your website. There are many more, of course, but these are often the main traffic sources for most law firm websites. In the "Other" category are paid directories and the like, and many attorneys may find that the bulk of their traffic comes from that "Other" category. If this is the case, then, as we discuss earlier in this book, it indicates that your website is not visible enough in Google.

Notice that social media is not in this graphic because it usually will not be a significant source of traffic to your website. Social media is important but for other reasons. Notice further that LinkedIn, while it is considered social media by many, is in this graphic because it can be a productive avenue for certain types of traffic.

Figure 35. Your Ecosystem's entry points.

It's worth noting that there are hundreds of millions of law-related searches each month in Google. My data shows that people are likely to start their law-related search in Google, often finding your other entry points through a Google search, as illustrated in the next figure, before they find your actual website.

The significance of Google as the entry point to your other entry points will be more evident as we continue this discussion.

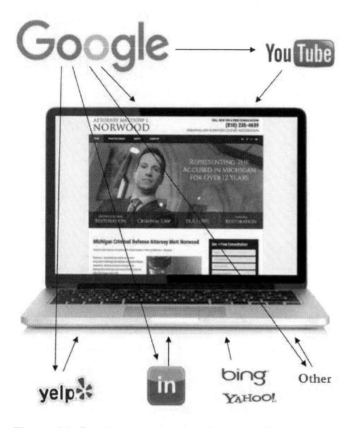

Figure 36. Google as an entry point into all other entry points of your Ecosystem.

Productive entry points are paramount because in lead generation, your website needs to have a lot of people who need legal help accessing it. Getting the maximum amount of traffic through your entry points is the outcome of your website's (and more generally, your Ecosystem's) online visibility. The more visible you are, especially in Google, the more likely people will enter your website.

Some entry points are high-volume and critical pathways, again, primarily Google. Others can be lower on your "to do" list, to get to when other more important development is underway. We discuss later some of these low-traffic, low-value entry points.

Points of Engagement

Unlike entry points, a point of engagement is a channel where someone subscribes to listen to you through "Likes" and as "Followers." Until they unsubscribe from your social media feed(s), it gives you an opportunity to shape your brand and to keep your law firm's name in their minds should they or a friend ever need legal assistance. In addition, your subscribers can make direct contact with you - and you can communicate directly back to them. Points of engagement include social media, YouTube and Yelp.

All of the media have some value because we want to push our message out to people through the media with which they are most comfortable.

A few of your engagement points serve other roles in your Ecosystem as well. For examples, Yelp, YouTube and LinkedIn are shown here as a point of engagement as well as in the previous "entry point" illustrations.

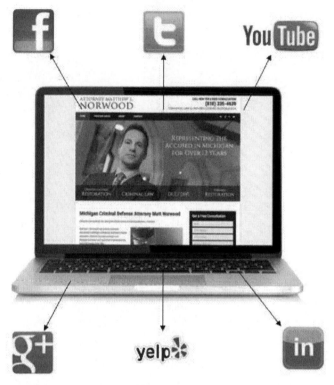

Figure 37. Your Ecosystem's points of engagement.

It's important to understand that a point of engagement is vital as a way to communicate with people who may someday need your services or know someone who does. However, a point of engagement is not to be viewed as a significant entry point, nor necessarily as a supporting element (more on supporting elements in the next section), both of which have different purposes in your ecosystem.

Some channels serve multiple roles in your Ecosystem but are most useful for one, sometimes two, roles. For example, Facebook, including Facebook advertising, is a low-value entry point but a particularly high-value point of engagement as well as a high-value supporting element.

To look at it in a different way, if you post a lot to Facebook expecting traffic to your website through that platform, you will be disappointed because it's a low-value entry point. However, if you post to Facebook knowing that its primary purpose is to engage with Facebook users with a secondary purpose of establishing trust and meeting the expectations of people coming to your website (i.e., a "supporting element"), then you can appreciate the value that it has in the Ecosystem and prioritize it accordingly.

Supporting Elements

Supporting elements are important to your Ecosystem development efforts because they make your website more productive as a lead generator. A supporting element helps a visitor to your website decide to make contact with you rather than one of your competitors. Videos are an example of a supporting element to your website. Videos help people connect visually with you, helping them to get to know the people behind the website. The connection so established will hopefully increase their comfort level before making their first contact with you.

As other examples of supporting elements, your blog helps establish your expertise in your practice areas and your social media gives your website personality and increases your credibility.

The illustration, below, depicts your website visitors on your website, reading your content and considering your supporting elements to decide whether you are the right lawyer for them.

Figure 38. Your Website's supporting elements.

Your YouTube channel, where all of your videos are located, is also a point of engagement and at this time is a lowish-value entry point, but your videos are an extremely important supporting element. As such, you can produce your videos knowing their role as a supporting element in your Ecosystem, without expecting outcomes for which the media is unsuited (such as being a source of a large amount of traffic to your website).

Your fully developed Ecosystem is shown in the following figure. See a larger version of this graphic in Appendix D.

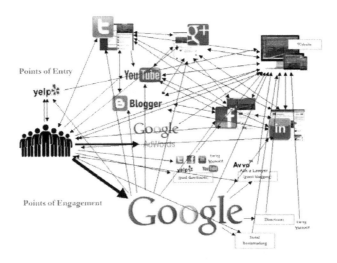

Figure 39. Your fully developed Ecosystem.

Chapter 7. Your Website As Your Ecosystem's Core

The Two Types of Law Firm Websites

Generally speaking, there are two broad categories of attorney websites although most websites are a combination of both. First, there is a "brochure" type website which is used by law firms that receive most of their clientele through their referral networks. Prospective clients who have been referred to the firm will go to the brochure website to learn more about the law firm before making initial contact.

The second type of website is the lead generator. The purpose of this website is to be visible in the search engines and to reach out to people in order to motivate them to make contact with the law firm.

The reason the distinction is important is because these websites vary a great deal in their appearance, structure, and content. This chapter focuses on the elements that will improve your law firm website as a lead generator.

An optimal website for your law firm has all of its supporting elements in place, or at least as many as you have the time and energy to produce, keeping in mind that some elements are more important than others. For example, your blog and Facebook Fan Page may be extremely important to reach your ideal clients, whereas it is joked that Google+ can be safely ignored unless your ideal client is a Google employee.

All of your Ecosystem, when taken together as a whole, is in an effort to give legal consumers a view of you and your law practice to convince them that you are the attorney with whom they need to make contact.

This chapter describes what makes up a good website as the core of your Internet Ecosystem. Then we go into more detail about several important supporting elements.

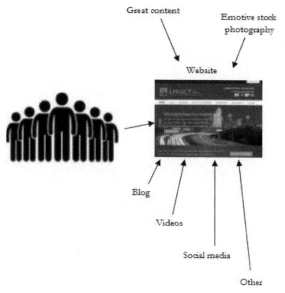

Figure 40. Your Website as your Ecosystem's core.

So first, we get a great website in place. The we begin developing your Ecosystem's supporting elements.

As you develop your supporting elements, such as your blog, social media and videos, we will commence with our online visibility efforts to get as many people into your Ecosystem as possible. We discuss the cultivation of your entry points more in later chapters.

And during the course of your Ecosystem development and traffic generation, you will start creating and maintaining various points of engagement, primarily, your social media.

Your Law Firm's Website

As we've mentioned before, at the core of your Ecosystem is your law firm's website, and the mobile version of your website, that will usually be the point of contact for people who need your help. Whether the online consumer chooses to make contact with you or not depends in large part on how they respond to your website's content - its look, feel and ease of use, bolstered by its supporting elements.

Components of a successful website

It is important to consider how effective your website will be in getting people to want to make contact with you through it. You can bring thousands of visitors to an underperforming website and have very little to show for it at the end of the month.

We discussed earlier in this book that with the right website you should expect between 10% and 15% of your website visitors to want to make contact with you when they reach it. Your anecdotal referral source information, as well as your Analytics and Google advertising data, should give you some idea whether your website is performing to expectations.

Modern design

Your website should be in accord with modern design trends. An archaic-looking website without a version formatted for mobile devices will look unprofessional to many. People respond much better to a modern website that looks great on their smart phones, Kindles, iPads, and PCs.

Figure 41. An example of a legal website that generates a high percentage of client inquiries.

Limited, predictable navigational choices

Your website should be easy for the visitor to navigate to the content they want. Simple, easy-to-use navigation throughout your website is key because you do not know which page on your website will be the visitor's entry page. Google will not always serve up the homepage of a website when it is deciding which pages in its index are most relevant to the legal consumer's query.

Logos, phone numbers and links should be in expected locations so that people don't have to search around for desired content. When people cannot find what they're looking for in the expected location (for example, your phone number in the top right part of your banner), in website user behavior studies, this is referred to as a "cognitive barrier." The idea is that people give up easily on a website when they are required to think about where something is located.

In addition to presenting our information and navigation in expected locations to avoid cognitive barriers, we need to limit the visitor's navigational choices to prevent "cognitive overload." This term refers to people leaving a website because they are required to think too much about their choices.

A famous study focusing on buying choices in a grocery store determined that a smaller number of available choices led to the largest number of products sold. Professors Sheena Iyengar and Mark Lepper published the study, "Why Choice is Demotivating," which disputes the popular notion that having more choices is the best sales strategy. They discovered that buyers are more likely to purchase products (in this instance, jams and chocolates) in a store when offered a smaller number of choices in product variety. Customers bought more when offered six varieties than when they were offered 24 or 30. Scientists refer to it as "choice overload."[11]

Figure 42. Limiting top navigational choices to six or fewer.

I believe that the findings of this study have a broader application to websites. Fewer navigational choices are better for keeping people on your website and our best performing websites have been built or modified with this principle in mind. It is recommended to keep above-the-fold navigational choices to around six or seven, with at least one of them, of course, being "Contact Us."

Easy-to-read content

Often the content of attorneys' websites is very informative but doesn't speak directly on an emotional level to a person who is looking to hire an attorney. Information-heavy content may be beneficial to people who are searching the web for legal information, but to reach people who are ready to hire, the content should be tailored to appeal to their immediate needs and likely mental state.

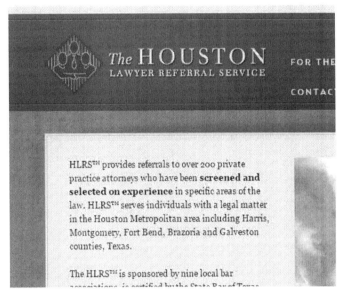

Figure 43. Easy-to-read typography, in this case, Georgia font, 12px.

Your pages should speak to the likely circumstances and frame of mind of your typical client, speaking to their probable preferences when hiring a lawyer for their type of legal problem. For example, if you are a family lawyer, your content might be warm and friendly because that client type may be looking for a caring, compassionate type of attorney. If you are a criminal defense attorney, your content might be more serious because that client type may be looking for a hard-as-nails litigator. As a defense lawyer, you might include in your content words like "tough" and "driven."

If your law practice relates to workplace injuries, rather than have your practice area page read like a textbook about workers compensation law, it should reach out to the injured employee, how stressful it can be to be out of work and how hard it can be to support a family while injured.

We also need to be mindful of generational differences. It's been found that "Millennials," millions of whom are already in their late-30s, often are more moved by information about what you do in the community and why you became a lawyer, rather than where you went to law school and how long you have been practicing law.

Make sure you use easy-to-understand language. Some believe that your content she be easy to comprehend by someone who reads at the level of a 9th grader.

One other audience you're writing for is your state's licensing authority, so your website content must comply with your local rules of professional conduct. I will discuss the ethics considerations of your online content in Chapter 15.

Appealing photography

The importance of good photography cannot be overstated. People will decide whether they want to stay on your website in a period lasting 3 to 5 seconds and engaging photography can help keep them there.

Photos of law books, gavels and scales of justice have been done to death and offer little visual interest anymore. If any of the images below look familiar to you, it is suggested that you remove them in favor of something that will provide more visual interest and will resonate for the visitor who comes to your website with a specific legal issue.

Figure 44. Examples of clichéd stock photography.

But if you have a criminal defense page, a photo of a row of police cars can make a difference. Likewise with family law, in place of that overused photo of the courthouse steps, include a photo of a little girl and you should find fewer people "bouncing"[12] from that page.

Following are a few examples of compelling stock photography from the Houston Lawyer Referral Service website (www.hlrs.org).

Figure 45. Sample image relating to family law.

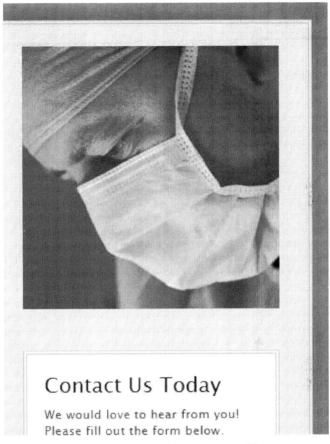

Figure 46. Sample image relating to personal injury.

A good profile picture of yourself and other lawyers in your firm can do a lot to personalize your website. An eye-tracking study of LinkedIn users found that the profile photo received the most viewing time. The study concluded that the profile photo was the single most important element on the LinkedIn profile page,[13] garnering 19% of a LinkedIn user's attention.

GILMAN & BEDIGIAN, LLC
Trial Attorneys

Call Us Toll Free 24/7
(800) 529-6162

Home | About Our Firm | Your Case | Personal Injury Claims | Blog | Recommendations | Contact

Figure 47. The principals of a personal injury law firm featured prominently on the website's homepage.

If you have one, consider adding a professional staff photo to your website as a personalizing element. If you're a solo practitioner, get a professional photo of yourself if you can and feature it prominently on your website.

Practice area-specific content

Often a law firm's website will have a practice areas page with bullet points listing its various areas of law. For Google and for your website visitor, it is ideal to have specific content relating to each subject area that is important to your law practice.

There are several good reasons to build out your practice area pages, and we talk about other reasons in Chapters 11 and 12. In the context of getting visitors to reach out to you once they get to your website, you should create pages for the practice areas that pertain to your website's ideal visitors specific legal issues.

You can create a large number of practice area pages for most areas of law if you have the staff resources and inclination. For example, if you have a family law practice area page, you can sub-divide it into separate pages for every type of family law case that you would like to take, including divorce, custody, child support, alimony, adoption, prenuptials, surrogacy and so on.

Very specific content is more likely to show in Google's search results and be the entry page of your website for the visitor performing that type law-related search. In this example, if someone searches for "medical malpractice lawyers in San Francisco," Google may put your page on the first page of its search results because your content is relevant to the search.

Medical Malpractice Lawyers in SF | Bar Association of San ...
www.sfbar.org/lawyerreferrals/med... ▾ The Bar Association of San Francisco ▾
If you or a loved one has been seriously injured because of negligence or error by a
medical professional, we can find a medical malpractice lawyer for your ...

Figure 48. Bar Association of San Francisco LRIS in third spot of Google's search results for "medical malpractice lawyers."

When a Google user clicks on that result, Google takes them directly to the malpractice page on BASF's website. That person is more likely to reach out to the legal service provider because they'll feel like they have found the resource they have been looking for.

Figure 49. Bar Association of San Francisco medical malpractice page.

Translate your website, or at least a page or two, into other languages spoken in your office and community.

If you want to reach groups in your community who are searching on the web for legal help in a language other than English, and you have a bi-lingual person on staff who can take those calls, Google will favor your translated content in it's search results and legal consumers will appreciate the effort.

Make the content easy to find in case someone accidentally finds themselves on the English-language part of your website.

Figure 50. Conspicuous top navigational link to Spanish content.

Testimonials

When allowed by your state,[14] testimonials from prior satisfied clients can do a lot to increase the comfort level of people coming to your website. If you have a particularly strong testimonial, consider using it as a call-out on multiple pages with a link that says, "Read more testimonials."

Lawyer Referral & Information Service
Client Testimonials

Client Testimonials

To request a referral, contact us by phone or online.

"...renewed my faith in attorneys! He (the attorney) was very informative and very easy to talk to. I wish there were more like him. I appreciate your services very much" - Laverne B.

Figure 51. One of many testimonials on the Bar Association of San Francisco website.

Do not limit your testimonials to the obvious "They were great" messages. Be creative with what people send to you in emails. On my website, one of the testimonials reads, *"Ken, you're fabulous! I like it that I can call you five times in a single day and you don't mind."*

Case results

As with testimonials, for certain practice areas, in particular personal injury, case results can appeal to the result-oriented website visitor. You will need to do some research to see if case results are allowed in your state. [15]

Conspicuous calls to action

You never want to leave a website visitor stranded on your page, unsure of what to do next. Calls to action above the scroll bar and elsewhere on the page can be very helpful in getting people to make contact with you. For example, buttons at the top and bottom of your pages saying something to the effect of "Contact us now for a free, no obligation consultation" can make a big difference in an otherwise poorly performing website.

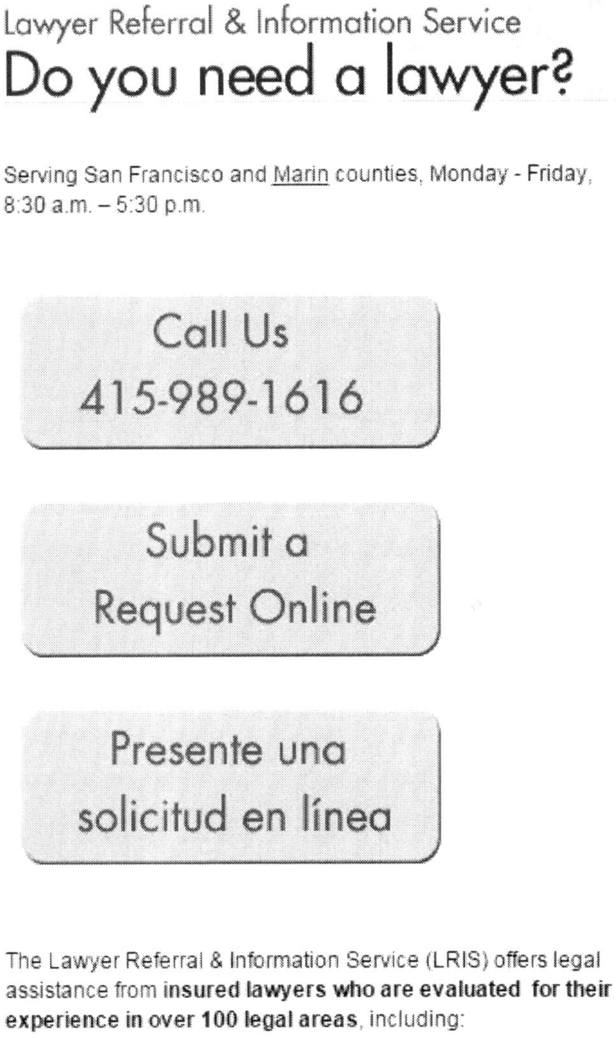

Lawyer Referral & Information Service

Do you need a lawyer?

Serving San Francisco and Marin counties, Monday - Friday,
8:30 a.m. – 5:30 p.m.

Call Us
415-989-1616

Submit a
Request Online

Presente una
solicitud en línea

The Lawyer Referral & Information Service (LRIS) offers legal
assistance from insured lawyers who are evaluated for their
experience in over 100 legal areas, including:

**Figure 52. Conspicuous calls to action on the BASF LRIS
website in the form of oversized buttons placed above the
main content.**

Figure 53. A right-sidebar contact form on every page of it's website.

Mobilize Your Website

The importance of having a mobile version of your website cannot be overstated.

Consider this:

- ComScore reports says smartphones and tablets account for 60 percent of all online traffic.[16]

- It was found that 61% of people have a better opinion of a brand when that company offers a good mobile experience.[17]

- Google announced that they disfavor non-mobile-ready websites in its mobile search results.

- Google announced that it has implemented a "mobile-first" index, which means that when indexing the content of the web, Google's spiders will go to the mobile version of the website first and index the desktop version of a website only if there is no mobile website in place.

- 88% of consumers conduct local searches on their smartphones and 18% of local searches lead to the purchase of products or services.[18]

The data shows that the smartphone is the preferred device by Google users to make contact with a law firm. If your website is not mobile-friendly, then many people who would be contacting you through their phones are not and you are missing out on a lot of inquiries.

In the following figure, you'll see a side-by-side comparison of two heavily trafficked legal websites in metropolitan areas of roughly comparable size. In this chart, the darker bars to the left of each comparison are 2014 inquiries to a legal website that does not have a version of its website formatted for mobile phones and the lighter bars are for a legal website that does have a version of its website formatted for phone.

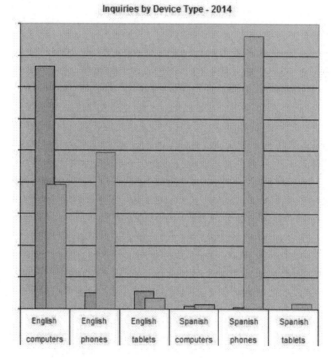

Figure 54. Inquiries to legal websites by device type.

Compare the dark and light bars in the column marked "English phones." When people are searching in Google in the English language, the mobile phone inquiries to with website with the mobile version of its website vastly outperforms the legal website without the mobile version.

The non-mobile website outperforms the mobile-ready legal website in the category "English computers," but these are email inquiries, not phone calls where the legal consumer gets to immediately communicate with the legal service provider.

When you compare the lighter bar for "English computers" with the darker bar for "English phones," it's clear that the mobile phone is the device of choice for people seeking legal help in Google.

A more dramatic example is seen in the category of "Spanish phones." For both websites, the "Spanish computers" inquiries are negligible. The presence of a mobile version of the legal website in Spanish makes the difference of whether the service provider is going to get any Spanish language inquiries at all. For the website without the mobile device, there are very few inquiries for the entire year, whereas for the mobile-ready website, Spanish language inquires exceed all other inquiry types.

I recognize that communities may vary somewhat by their local residents' search habits and devices of choice, but I'd say that the variations are probably not very much. For the 30 bar associations and scores of law firms for which I provide marketing services, the data is fairly consistent in every community for which I have significant data.

The conversion rate (i.e., the percentage of people who come to your website who choose to make contact with you) on mobile devices is impressive too.

While we expect people to reach out to lawyers at a rate of 10% to 15% through their websites, we often find that conversion rates[19] (how Google describes a smartphone) through the handheld versions of the website often exceed 25%. In the figure below, you'll notice that "Mobile devices with full browsers"[20] have conversion rates in excess of 30% and are responsible for most of this advertiser's inquiries. This data is drawn from six months of data from July 1, 2014 to December 31, 2014.

Device	Campaign	Bid adj. [?]	Converted ↓ clicks [?]	Click conversion rate [?]
Total			693	14.56%
Mobile devices with full browsers		+ 30%	331	38.99%
Mobile devices with full browsers		+ 30%	165	31.25%
Computers			83	4.44%
Mobile devices with full browsers		+ 30%	30	17.24%
Mobile devices with full browsers		+ 30%	24	42.11%
Computers			13	3.94%
Mobile devices with full browsers		+ 30%	13	18.06%

Figure 55. Conversion rate by device type.

Examples of two mobile websites that are over-performers are those of BASF and HLRS, shown in the next two figures.

In the first 6 months of 2015, the BASF LRIS mobile website converted at 33.53% for one of it's busiest Google advertising campaigns. To put that another way, one-third of the Google users who came to this mobile website made contact with BASF's LRIS. The conversion rate for the Spanish-language version of

BASF's mobile website is an astounding 45.92% over the same period (726 smartphone visitors from their Google advertising resulting in 332 phone calls).

The HLRS mobile website is a close second, converting at 31.87% for the first half of 2015 (1,300 smartphone visitors from their Google advertising resulting in 406 phone calls).

Note that both mobile websites have conspicuous click-to-call buttons. In the case of the HLRS mobile website, the user cannot scroll away from the click-to-call button.

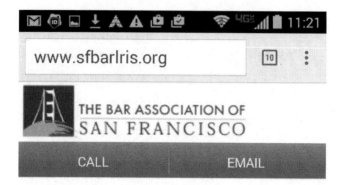

DO YOU NEED A LAWYER?

We can help!

» Attorneys: Learn about our program and how you can join

The Lawyer Referral & Information Service (LRIS) offers legal assistance from lawyers who are **pre-screened for their experience in over 100 legal areas**, including:

- Bankruptcy Law
- Business Law
- Criminal Law
- Disability Rights Law
- Elder Abuse/Benefit Claims
- Employment Law

Figure 56. BASF LRIS website as displayed on an Android smartphone.

Need a Houston Lawyer?

The Houston Lawyer Referral Service is a non-profit community service project of the legal profession that was established in 1958.

The HLRS™ is sponsored by nine local bar associations, is certified by the State Bar of Texas, and is one of a select few programs nationwide that meets the standards of the American Bar Association.

HLRS™ provides referrals to over 400 private practice attorneys who have been screened and selected on experience in specific areas of the law. HLRS™ serves individuals with a legal matter in the Houston Metropolitan area including Harris, Montgomery, Fort Bend, Brazoria and

Request a Lawyer Referral »

Call Us: (713) 237-9429

Figure 57. HLRS website as displayed on an Android smartphone.

If your website is on WordPress, there are plug-ins that will create a quick (and free) mobile version of your website. Results vary by website and it's not always pretty, but it's a good temporary fix while you're exploring other options. WPtouch is the WordPress plug-in we use in these circumstances.

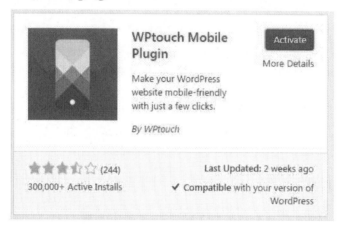

Chat software

Giving website visitors an additional way to reach you by instant message helps to personalize a website and lets visitors know that there are real people behind the website.

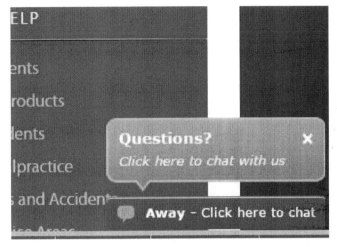

Figure 58. Inexpensive and easy to use chat software by Zopim (zopim.com).

Badges and Awards

If you have awards, recognitions or any other badges that can bolster your credibility and expertise, add them to your website. SuperLawyers, Martindale-Hubbell, Better Business Bureau, and other websites offer opportunities to get impressive third-party logos to improve your visitor's response rate.

Figure 59. Credibility bolstering accolades.

In the same way, if you support a local charity or cause, try to secure a logo for that cause to reach the significant number of legal consumers who care about your community involvement. This is referred to as "cause marketing."

Chapter 8. Your Website's Supporting Elements and Points of Engagement

This chapter discusses in more detail the elements in support of your website as well as the avenues of direct communication to legal consumers through your Ecosystem.

Your Website's Blog

Blogs on law firm websites are important for several reasons and law-related blogs have become commonplace.

The reason most cited for active blogging is that Google wants your content to be of high quality and expanding. Google often rewards you for the effort by moving your website higher up in its search results. We discuss this more in later chapters.

As a supporting element, having an active blog helps people decide to make contact with you. A frequently updated blog that is useful, interesting, and related to the consumer's legal concerns establishes your expertise, authority and if the tone is right, approachability. It also tells visitors that there are real lawyers behind the website, knowledgeable and wanting to help.

As a point of engagement, when the blog is set up to allow it, people can subscribe to your blog, which makes it possible to push your posts out to them until the unsubscribe.

I would like to emphasize here that the word "active" is a critical part of the phrase, "having an active blog." Have you ever clicked on the blog link to find three or four posts from 2011 and nothing since? It gives the impression that the lights are on but no one is home.

Your YouTube Channel

It's not widely known that YouTube is the second largest search engine in the world. If your videos show high in the search results, users are more likely to find you and reach out to you, perhaps navigating to your website through your YouTube channel or possibly making contact with you directly through it. We discuss this more later when we consider YouTube as a traffic source.

As a supporting element, a well-developed YouTube channel can be a terrific supporting element to your website. By having videos on subject matters relating to your practice areas and about your firm, several benefits accrue. First, as a supporting element, it gives a face and voice to your law firm. For example, if you have a video as a simple introduction to your firm, it gives people an opportunity to get to know you before they make their first contact.

In an earlier chapter, we discussed how online consumers can be intimidated by the attorney-hiring process. By giving users an opportunity to meet you and your staff through a video, it can help the rate at which consumers make contact with you through your website.

Figure 60. YouTube video featuring the lawyers and staff of the law firm.

Remember that we have the ultimate goal of getting fifteen percent of the users who come to your website to use your contact form, click to call, or pick up the telephone and dial. When you make a video on a specific topic, you can embed that video into your website on a page that makes sense. For example, if you have a video about child support, you can embed that video in your child support page. People can see you talking on that topic before your first contact; and you have established your approachability and expertise in advance. The right video can make a positive difference in an otherwise lackluster website.

As YouTube continues to grow as a search engine for millions of Americans, there's no time like the present to set up a YouTube channel for your law firm to increase its visibility to people who are searching for law-related video content.

This section is about YouTube as a supporting element but in fact, YouTube serves in all three capacities in your Ecosystem:

YouTube serves as a point of engagement as well. When people subscribe to your channel then your are able to engage directly with them through the publication of new videos, push your expanding video content out to them for as long as they stay subscribed.

Implementation of your YouTube channel

Often it is difficult for lawyers to get started in YouTube. While the setup of a YouTube channel is straightforward and is now integrated with your Gmail account, the production of videos is more challenging.

I take the approach of "better fast than perfect." If it's easier for you to produce videos in-house rather than hiring an outside videographer, and if that will help you create five or ten videos quickly, then that is the preferred approach. Sufficiently high-quality videos can be produced with an inexpensive video camera, good lighting, and a microphone that you can buy from Amazon for very little money. Good sound and reasonable lighting are key.

Then if you can find someone who can put a title at the beginning, introducing you and the subject matter of the video, and a call to action at the end, you have a video for your YouTube channel to be streamed back to your website. Don't forget disclaimers at the end.

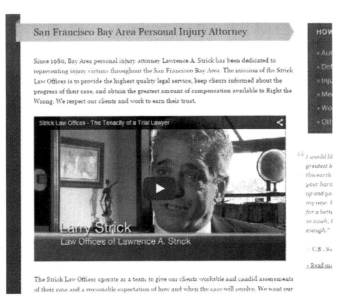

Figure 61. YouTube video embedded into a homepage.

Your video does not have to be very long. If it's only 60 seconds in length, that can be sufficient.

If you are not sure what the content of your video can be, simply read a paragraph off of your website that is the subject matter of the video. For example, you can read a paragraph about child support off of your child support page, a paragraph about your firm from your "About Us" page, or an introduction to your law firm off of the home page.

Your Social Media Platforms

Well-developed social media presence enhances your credibility with Google as "trust factors," especially Google+. Google indexes all of the four major social media platforms and there's evidence that it favors websites that have active social media.

Google and Twitter entered into a deal early in 2015 giving Google much more access to Twitter users' feeds. This has allowed Google to index Twitter accounts and display Tweets in Google's search results in real time.

Through your growing number of followers, you can increase awareness of your firm among the thousands of social media users in your community.

Social media as supporting elements

An astonishingly large number of people use social media. As adoption of the platforms becomes nearly universal, the major social media platforms are vital brand-management tools.[21] Active social media is a crucial supporting element in the effort to maximize the number of online visitors who choose to make contact with you through your web presence.

Your social media is not just limited to your Facebook Fan Page and your Twitter account, although those are most important. A LinkedIn Company Page can help build out your network of referral sources with other attorneys and cultivate connections with other professionals who may someday need your services.

Here are a few more reasons for maintaining active social media.

Social media makes your website dynamic

As a supporting element, frequently updated social media makes your website more dynamic and lets people know that yours is not just a static website that was published a long time ago and forgotten.

People like them

In a study relating to how consumers interact with a retail website, it was found that consumers purchased 25% more often on websites that had social media icons,[22] whether they clicked on them or not. People have come to expect the icons, and you will even see Facebook and Twitter icons on collateral material like brochures and billboards.

Lots of social media connections are votes in your favor. Nothing says credibility, authority and trustworthiness to your website visitors like hundreds of "Likes" and "Followers" to your social media feeds.

EETS   FOLLOWING   FOLLOWERS
39   244   761

veets   Tweets & replies

Figure 62. Credibility established through Twitter followers.

You can shape your brand

A large number of followers allows you to talk to your community and actively shape your "brand" (or re-shape it). It also affords an opportunity to respond to what people are saying about your law firm, positive or negative.

It's helpful

"Followers" sometimes ask questions and your thoughtful responses will be remembered.

Social Media as Points of Engagement

Social media's prime function is to be a point of engagement for all legal consumers who opt-in to listen to your message. In the cases of a Twitter "Follower" and Facebook "Like," the social media user has in effect given you permission to publish content to their social media accounts on any topic you'd like until they opt-out by un-Following you on Twitter and un-Liking you on Facebook, and so on.

Implementation

The construction of a set of integrated social media accounts—Facebook Fan Page, Google+ business page, Twitter, and LinkedIn Company Page—and a consistent banner and profile images across all social media platforms will create a unified presence and brand for your law firm.

Icons for the four (or five - Pinterest?) social media platforms should be featured prominently on your website, inviting website visitors to visit you at your various online locations.

Figure 63. Conspicuous social media icons using a free script from AddThis (www.addthis.com).

"Share" links make it possible for website visitors to share your content through their social media platforms to their "Friends" and "Followers" helping you to further engage with social media users.

Figure 64. Free left-margin share buttons from AddThis.

Links back to your site should be prominently featured on the four platforms and included occasionally in media posts to the extent possible without being off-putting to your followers. This way people who find you first on one of your social media platforms can easily navigate to your website to learn more about your service.

Your Yelp listing

A Yelp profile with lots of positive reviews can be a terrific supporting element to your website. It has been found that 85% of consumers trust online reviews as much as they do personal recommendations from friends, relatives and colleagues.

As a supporting element, if your Yelp profile has many reviews and you have 4 or 5 stars, it will help many Yelp users decide to make contact with you.

Another reason why a well-developed Yelp profile with lots of good reviews is important is because Yelp often appears high in Google's search results. If someone is looking for your law firm by name, there is a possibility that in addition to your website and your Google Maps listing, your firm's Yelp profile will feature prominently in the search results.

If your Yelp reviews are bad, your inquiry rate will suffer. In that case, you'll want to claim your Yelp listing, put in positive information about your law firm, as well as appealing photos of you, your staff and your office, and start hustling for 5-star reviews from former satisfied clients. We'll get into that more in a later chapter.

Yelp is not point of engagement because it only allows you a few limited options to communicate, publicly or privately, with individual reviewers and no way to push new content to a wider audience of Yelp users.

We will talk about the importance of positive reviews (as of summer 2017, especially Google+ reviews), how to get them, and dealing with negative reviews in later chapters, including ethics issues relating to eliciting reviews with too much specificity.

Chapter 9. Your Website's Entry Points

People need to be able to find your website if you are going to get leads from it. To make it more visible, there are a variety of things you can do. For example, you could advertise in Google and/or Bing, and you can optimize your website towards the goal of getting it to rank higher in the search engines' indices. You may have one or more social media profiles and maybe you're posting listings for your services on legal classified websites.

If you're engaged in some of these visibility efforts, you know that they are time-consuming and can be expensive. However, there are sources of traffic that deliver more than other sources for the same expenditure of effort. We naturally want to focus on the most productive of these if we have limited resources.

Traffic Through Google

The majority of your website traffic should be coming from Google because that's where the largest portion of law-related search originates. Now we'll get into how to get as many Google users to your website as possible.

Google advertising

With Google's staggering volume of law-related search activity, Google's Sponsored Listings for most lawyers will likely be the most productive source of leads. If your website is visible in the organic results, you may already be getting a lot of traffic from Google. However, Google advertising will be a source of higher quality traffic because everyone we bring to our website through that channel is actively searching for legal help.

For example, in Google's organic search results, we may rank well for "damages in a wrongful death case" which makes our website an important information resource for people who are researching that topic. Yet through Google advertising, we can put ourselves at the top of Google's first page for "wrongful death lawyer," reaching people who are searching for legal help, not legal information.

A well-built Google account is vitally important to the overall success of Google advertising. Targeting thousands of search phrases and creating hundreds of narrowly focused ads ensures that you are casting the broadest possible net, thereby getting the maximum number of law-related click activity for your marketing investment.

Google advertising is effective because it gives you immediate first page visibility in Google's search results for every search you want. In addition, as we've mentioned elsewhere, it targets Google users who are looking for a lawyer right now.

Google Sponsored Listings is discussed more fully in later chapters.

Figure 65. The top four Sponsored Listings in Google's search results.

Google Remarketing

"Google Remarketing" is Google's name for cookie-based advertising. The idea is that when people come to your website, we hope for them to make contact with you around 15% of the time. What that means is that about 85% of the people who come to your website do not make contact with you on their first visit.

Through Google Remarketing, we plant a cookie on every visitor to your website, whether they make contact with you or not.

Figure 66. Example of a Google Remarketing ad.

Then every time Google detects that cookie on someone's browser when that person is visiting on of Google's millions of affiliated websites, Google shows one of your ads to them. This can be a graphical banner ad, a text ad, or a rotation of both. Your banners would vary in over a dozen dimensions to fit the requirements of the particular website. For example, Google may display one of your small banners across the bottom of a YouTube video, or Google may display a larger square banner on Yelp.[23]

Besides Yelp and YouTube, Google partners with millions of other websites, many of which are among the most heavily trafficked websites on the web, such as the New York Times, the Los Angeles Times and Pandora. Soon users get the impression that you've got the biggest advertising budget in the world because they can't get away from your ads.

People browsing the web with your cookie in tow will see your ads frequently and eventually may click on one of them. Sometimes on their second visit they will choose to make contact with you although they didn't the first time.

After you have been running your remarketing ads for a while, Google will have gathered enough information about your typical visitors and will make available a target group known as "Similar to" your remarketing list. This gives you the opportunity to show ads to people who have never been to your website before but have cookies that are similar to yours, quite possibly the cookie of a competing law firm in your community.

It's inexpensive too. The clicks are often under one dollar, which is a steal by Google advertising standards.

As one final noteworthy benefit of remarketing, a 2013 Harvard Business School study on display ads and search behavior found that exposure to a display ad increases the number of relevant search queries by as much as 25% and if the display ad is viewed within 10 minutes of the search, it can be as high as 45%.[24]

A recent unfortunate development is that Google is disabling this type of marketing for certain types of advertisers that sell services or products that are sensitive in nature. The application of this policy had been scattershot over the last 2 years but in December 2015, Google disabled some (but not all) of the remarketing advertising for criminal attorneys in my portfolio, as well as a few family law firms. One advertiser was a general practitioner yet had their cookies disabled because criminal defense was a small part of their advertising. I've also had cookies disabled for personal injury and bankruptcy.

Despite my best efforts on the phone with a Google policy representative, this is the result of a manual review and there is no appeal process. The policy is explicit and directly on point:

> *Commission of a Crime*
>
> *Sites or apps providing information, products, or services relating to alleged commission of crimes or crime convictions may not collect users for userlists. Commission of a crime content may include services targeted for alleged convictions, as well as general services such as criminal directories.*

They have similar policies against remarketing lists for other sensitive practice areas under this policy.

As of this writing, Google's execution of the new policy is somewhat arbitrary or random, and my firm still has other criminal defense, family law and medical malpractice remarketing campaigns running. We'll see how long it lasts and whether Google will extend this policy toward other types of law that may be perceived as "sensitive."

Google's "Call-only" campaigns

As we discuss elsewhere in this book, the appearance and usability of your website is an important first step towards getting the most from your online marketing investment. If your website isn't drawing people in like it should, then you may not be getting as many inquiries from your marketing investment as you could be.

In February 2015 Google made available a new type of advertising called "Call-only ads" and launched "Call-only campaigns" in June 2015. These campaigns allow you to advertise in Google only on smartphones without a mobile-formatted website – without a website at all, in fact. Further, when advertising to people who are searching for legal help in a language other than English, the new ad format eliminates the prerequisite of translating any of your website.

Here's how it works.

You create a special Call-only that looks something like this:

Call: (718) 624-0843
www.BrooklynBar.org/LRS
Referrals to Qualified Lawyers.
Trusted Since 1872. Call Now!

Figure 67. Example of a Call-only ad.

Like any search ad, you connect it to certain search phrases in your account and give Google your maximum bid - essentially telling Google the most you are willing to spend whenever someone calls your firm through the ad after typing in one of the phrases you're bidding on. But unlike regular Google ads, they display only on mobile phones and people who are moved to click on the ad have no choice other than to call you. They cannot click through to your website.

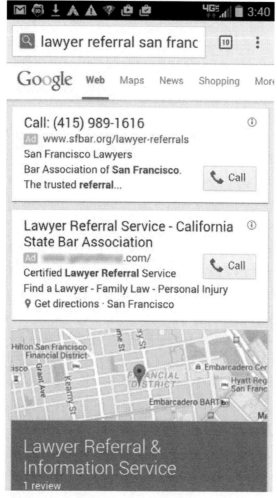

Figure 68. Call-only ad as it shows on a smartphone.

The figure above shows what the Call-only ad looks like on a smartphone for the search "lawyer referral san francisco." Notice how it differs from the second ad which is a text ad with a call extension. In the case of the second ad, the legal consumer has the option to navigate to several pages on the website of the advertiser. Each click costs the advertiser according to its maximum bid (and a few other factors). In the Call-only ad, the advertiser pays only when someone calls the service.

What this means is that if you're running only these types of ads, you're getting calls through your Google advertising without the need for a good website. You can also run these ads in Spanish and get calls from Spanish-speaking consumers, again without translating a single word of your website!

Other benefits of the Call-only ad.

Besides eliminating the need to upgrade, update, mobilize and/or translate your website in advance of advertising it, there are other benefits to this type of advertising.

Scheduling.

You can schedule the ads to run during the hours of the day when you have the ability to actually answer the phone. If your office closes for lunch, you can schedule the ads to be paused for that hour. If your office is closed for the afternoon for a staff meeting or you're in trial, you can paused the ads and not squander a single dollar of your marketing budget on an unanswerable call.

And if you have a Spanish speaker on staff who is maybe part-time, you can schedule the Spanish language versions of the ads to run only during the hours when that staff person is available the phone.

You're reaching people on their p

As shown in an earlier figure, my people are much more likely to ma your firm through their mobile phones than by email. For Spanish-language Google users, the mobile phone as a contact method is practically to the exclusion of PCs and tablets.

This is a phone call from someone actively searching for legal help.

In normal Google advertising, you pay Google when someone clicks on one of your ads whether they contact you or not. In this case, you pay Google only when someone actually calls you. There is no downside – if no Google user clicks on it, you pay nothing, and everyone who does click on it is calling you for help.

People actually click on these ads.

We've been running Call-only ads for many law firms since the new ad format was introduced, and these ads have caused thousands of consumers to directly call our advertisers, at an average phone call price of roughly what a regular search click costs. Each one of these callers saw the ad after performing a search on their phone for legal help.

Paid advertising doesn't get cheaper and more targeted than that.

ETHICS ALERT

If you are advertising in Google and your ads have click-to-call functionality (which they should), there was an unfortunate development for advertisers in the United States.

In November 2017, Google started randomly monitoring and recording phone calls, ostensibly "to evaluate and improve the quality of" its advertising programs. Google promises that none of the information will be tied to any specific individual and that it will be aggregated for statistical purposes. Each call through a Google ad will begin with something like "This call may be monitored or recorded by Google for quality assurance purposes."

All ads with call extensions that existed before November 6, 2017 are grandfathered in with the monitoring, but if you ever want to edit the ads or create new ads, Google requires that you consent to the monitoring.

I see this as possibly compromising the attorney-client privilege and can be an issue for lawyers, doctors and other professionals who handle sensitive information.

Google allows for an exemption for information protected by HIPAA and as of this writing, I'm trying to get Google to provide a similar exemption for attorney-client privileged communications, so far fruitlessly.

In the meantime, if someone says they found you in a Google search and you think it may have been one of your ads, it's suggested that you call them back so that Google doesn't have an opportunity to listen in on sensitive information.

Google's "organic" results

Search engine optimization (SEO) is activity you do for the purpose of getting Google to favor your website in its natural listings. The Sponsored Listings, discussed above, will bear immediate fruit and SEO is a longer, more deliberate process. Over time, if your visibility efforts are successful, "Google organic" should be showing as the largest single source of traffic in your analytics data.

Ideally, your website should be in the Sponsored Listings, the maps results and in the organic results through SEO, and because of its importance, we dedicate a chapter later in this book to the mechanics of SEO.

Traffic through Bing and Yahoo

There are two other search engines that we need to talk about: - Bing and Yahoo. While Google's law-related search traffic is by far the greatest among these three search engines, the type of consumer you reach in Bing and Yahoo is similar to the legal consumer searching in Google, only in smaller numbers and less likely to be on a smartphone.

For search engine optimization, I have found that what works for Google optimization has comparable effects on your rankings in Bing and Yahoo. Therefore, we can keep our optimization efforts focused on Google and hope for the best for these lower-volume search engines.

As for advertising, Bing has modeled their advertising platform and ad delivery system entirely on Google's. Bing has even made it possible to import your Google account directly into your Bing account.

I have found the clicks to be cheaper in Bing than in Google, but I have found that the inquiry rate is lower, which is puzzling. I usually recommend against Bing advertising unless you are already spending enough in Google to have at least a 90% impression share.[25]

As of this writing, Yahoo advertising is in a state of flux, which hints at shifting priorities and/or confusion within the company. Under a deal with Bing, Yahoo is to deliver at least half of its desktop ads from Bing itself, so if you're advertising in Bing, you're advertising in Yahoo too without realizing it.

Later in 2015, Yahoo also entered into a deal with Google to display Google ads some of the 50% of the time that are not serving up Bing ads. Meanwhile, also late in 2015, Yahoo was pushing its own advertising platform known as Yahoo Gemini, which is intended to serve ads when Yahoo is not delivering the ads of its two competitors. I have not as of this writing had a chance to use Yahoo Gemini advertising. I've found its interface incomplete and nearly impossible to work within, so there's no data in my possession that would allow me to conclude whether Gemini works or not for legal advertising.

Traffic Through Yelp

Earlier we discuss your law firm's Yelp profile as a supporting element in a well-developed web presence. We are revisiting Yelp here as a source of traffic.

We must note at the outset that, despite what their salespeople tell you, Yelp is not a search engine for legal services.

It may be a search engine for hotels, hair cutters and restaurants because the information you need to know about each of those business types is limited basically to location, price and customer satisfaction. All of that information is readily available in Yelp and you can easily make your choice about where you're eating tonight or where you will be staying on your next business trip.

But imagine we only wanted to go to a restaurant where the chef went to a top culinary academy. Imagine further that it was important for us that the restaurant owners engaged in community activities to help the less fortunate. If this were the case, we probably wouldn't start our search in Yelp because there's no point in reading reviews for a bunch of restaurants not knowing which of them meet our other selection criteria.

Hiring a lawyer is a bigger decision than deciding where to eat today and consequently, more important selection criteria than location, price and customer satisfaction are at play.

That said, when Yelp users are comparing profiles, they are very likely to be at the point in their decision-making process that they are ready to hire you. Therefore, it's important that your Yelp profile be up to the task once they have decided to read what your previous clients have said about you.

There's more about managing your Yelp profile in a later chapter.

Yelp advertising

Yelp advertising is akin to other pay-per-click advertising models like Google, except that you bid on categories like "Lawyers" rather than specific search phrases like "Chicago family lawyers downtown."

An "Enhanced Profile" gives you the ability to showcase your unique selling points, reach out to Yelp users in a more direct way, and remove competitors' ads from your profile.

By advertising, you get the top spot in the search results whereas otherwise your profile, if one exists at all, is often buried among other legal service providers and law firms.

Figure 69. Top placement in Yelp's search results through Yelp advertising.

Only a few ads are displayed per search, and the ads themselves integrate well into the normal search results, appearing to be a natural search result.

I've always disfavored Yelp advertising because I figure that there are generally three reasons why someone would be in Yelp:

(1) Validation of a business that they know about and are considering hiring,

(2) As a search engine - looking for a reputable business when they don't know one yet, or

(3) Reading funny reviews.

With Yelp advertising, we're trying to reach group (2) only, because group (1) will find you regardless, and group (3) would be bored to death reading your 5-star reviews. I don't know how big group (2) is, but I'd wager that the largest group is (1), unless we're talking about restaurants and hotels, in which case group (2) is probably the largest group.

Here are the pros and cons as I see them:

Pros:

(A) If you have a strong Yelp profile, it's good to show it off to group (2), even if it's a small group.

(B) When people in group (2) are reading reviews, it's a reasonable supposition that they're considering hiring your law firm (group (1) too, but you don't need to advertise to get them to your profile).

Cons:

(C) The clicks are more expensive than one would expect.

(D) We have no control over how much a click cost, nor can we control scheduling and specific geographic targeting.

(E) There's no transparency on how the money is spent - Yelp pretty much just tells you when the money is used up.

(F) There are no meaningful reports that would make it easy to track ROI.

(F) We spend click money needlessly on groups (1) and (3).

> WARNING: In any case, I recommend that you do not run Yelp ads if you have a rating of fewer than 4-stars (it as been found that 92% of Yelp users are satisfied with that many). If you have no reviews at all, maybe try it. If you have a lot of negative reviews, you should consider taking the opposite approach of keeping it as invisible as possible until you've had a chance to get your star-rating higher with more 5-star reviews.

I still run Yelp ads for my clients when they get coupons for free advertising (usually in the $100 to $300 range). In locations where I've run Yelp ads, I find that Google clicks are cheaper and have many more targeting options.

That said, for a limited run on a Yelp coupon, "free" is a good price. Yelp appears to send out a lot of coupons offering a free introductory run with no commitment to continue. If you've received an email like the following from Yelp, I encourage you to give it a shot and pause it when you reach your coupon limit. Yelp will require a credit card but if you keep your total budget within the amount of the coupon, you're good.

Figure 70. Yelp advertising promotion.

After your free coupon runs out, if you're finding like I did that the cost per click in your community is north of $10 per click, I continue to recommend against Yelp advertising. Google will deliver more visitors for the price and the Google visitors will be coming to your website, not just to your Yelp profile.

Traffic Through Social Media Marketing

Earlier in this book we discuss social media as important supporting elements and points of engagement. It should be understood that social media functions mainly in those roles.

Your social media platforms will not by themselves be a significant source of traffic except through social media advertising.

Facebook advertising

If you have a Facebook Fan Page for your law firm, you have an opportunity to put advertisements into Facebook users' personal pages as "Sponsored Posts."

Figure 71. An example of a Facebook Sponsored Post from my company.

It is unclear at this time whether any quality traffic can be brought to your law firm's website through this type of advertising. You can target Facebook users according to certain demographics like age, location, and interests, none of which we have found especially helpful for attorneys. As of now, Facebook does not allow advertisers to target keywords like Twitter does. It's a curious shortcoming that hopefully they'll address someday.

Keyword targeting would allow an advertiser to sponsor a post when someone has matching words on their Facebook page. As an example, if you wanted to promote a post from your Facebook Fan Page about your personal injury practice, keyword targeting would allow us to show that post only when someone has the words "injury" or "injury lawyer" and the like on their page.

On the other hand, Facebook advertising is currently an inexpensive source of traffic. Its best use for me is that it makes it possible to insert Google Remarketing cookies onto the browsers of Facebook users when they visit your website from a Facebook ad.

For my own company, I occasionally use Facebook advertising to raise awareness of the Facebook Fan page itself, accumulate "Likes" or to highlight a specific post. Having no expectation of receiving any quality traffic from Facebook advertising, I have not been disappointed when I find that I haven't.

In May 2015, Facebook made it possible to insert a "Call Now" button into your Facebook sponsored posts allowing people accessing Facebook on their

smartphones to directly click to call the advertiser. I don't have enough data to say whether the "Call Now" buttons help in any significant way.

I recommend against Facebook for lead generation because of its overly broad demographics and lack of keyword targeting.

LinkedIn advertising

LinkedIn offers a few different ways to advertise to a demographically targeted group. The demographic targeting in LinkedIn advertising allows you to narrow your audience down to industry type, job title, and geographic location. As primarily a networking website for professionals, we have found it to be a productive way to connect with an attorney's network of referral sources. It can be productive as a lead generator for attorneys who represent other professionals or small businesses.

 Lawyers: Need Clients? Over 1 Billion Law-Related Google Ads Served! Learn How We Can Help.

Figure 72. Example of my company's LinkedIn ad.

LinkedIn advertising is getting more competitive and expensive. Several years ago my company was paying about three dollars per click and currently we're paying about nine dollars per click.

Twitter advertising

If you have a Twitter account setup for your law firm, you can advertise in the form of "Promoted Tweets" and "Website Cards." Unlike Facebook advertising, Twitter does allow for keyword targeting. If you want to show "Promoted Tweets" in your community whenever someone posts a tweet containing the words "injury lawyer," this is possible in Twitter. The Twitter users see your ads based on the content of their tweets, whether or not that tweeter is a "Follower" of your Twitter account.

Ken Matejka @MatejkaMarketng   30 Jan 2015

Lawyers: Need Clients? Over 1 Billion Google Ads Served! Learn How We Can Help. Call Us at (415) 513-8736. cards.twitter.com/cards/18ce53x3...

Attorneys - Need More Clients Fast? Get Google Visibility in 3 Days!

matejkamarketing. com

Learn more

Figure 73. Example of Twitter-promoted Tweet with Card.

At this time Twitter advertising is inexpensive, about one dollar per click is what we're currently seeing.

Twitter advertising is good for its keyword targeting and it gives another opportunity to place cookies inexpensively into the browsers of your visitors when they come to your website. However, we haven't yet seen it prove its self as a source for clients. I'm lukewarm on this advertising medium until it proves itself as productive for legal service providers.[26]

As an entry point, Twitter can be, indirectly, a source of organic Google traffic. Since February 2015, Google gained complete access to Twitter streams. A

June 2015 unnamed Google algorithmic update, your Tweets can show up in Google search results following a law-related search, in theory anyway.

Traffic Through YouTube

In an earlier chapter we talk about YouTube as filling all three categories in your Ecosystem. We revisit YouTube here to talk more about it as a source of traffic to your website.

Aging Millennials are daily YouTube users and it is reported that there are over 6 billion hours of video viewed each month.[27]

A well-developed YouTube channel gives you an opportunity to be visible among the enormous number of people using YouTube as a search engine.

As for search engine optimization, YouTube continues to be the Wild West in terms of how simple it is to get your videos to rank well in its search results. Keyword-stuffing in the video file names, titles, descriptions, and tags is enough in many communities to get your videos to rank. In more competitive markets like NYC and LA, there are so many law firms who have been doing this for years that the SEO game is more challenging.

Notice that the video featured below has nearly 79,000 views, primarily through natural YouTube visibility efforts.

Figure 74. BASF LRIS YouTube video.

YouTube advertising

Through YouTube advertising, you can show one or more pre-selected videos to YouTube users. You can also facilitate the display of these videos on other websites with which Google has an association to run ads.

A prerequisite of YouTube advertising is having a good video. In the Fall of 2016, Google launched a new program called "YouTube Director" to help you create a video cheaply. More on that later in this book.

Once you have a video of reasonable quality to promote your legal services, YouTube is an inexpensive way to get your message in front of a lot of people. With a daily budget of $10 and maximum bid of $0.25, you can get a lot of views for about

$0.07 per view. Make the video less than 30 seconds in length if possible to reduce the number of people who opt to "Skip this ad." Ads of 10 to 15 seconds in length are growing more common and are harder for a YouTube user to skip.

Like Facebook and LinkedIn, YouTube advertising at this time is based on overly-broad demographic targeting like age and parental status, but it does allow an advertiser to target geographically. If you are using Google's cookie-based Remarketing advertising, you can set your YouTube ads to show only to YouTube users who have been to your website before or match the profile of people who have been to your website before.

Last year, YouTube advertising was integrated into the Google AdWords dashboard, making it easier to monitor than it had been when you had to log in to YouTube separately.

As of yet, we have had no concrete return on investment data from YouTube advertising, but I recommend it because it is so cheap. We run campaigns with a daily budget as low as $2 and get a lot of exposure for our attorneys and bar associations.

Paid Directory Listings

Some attorneys have reported to me that some paid directories result in good traffic while others I speak to about it are disappointed in the results when weighed against the costs.

Before you list in a paid directory, whether a small local directory, a practice area-specific directory or one of the major national directories, it's important to determine what that listing will bring you before you make any commitments and start spending your marketing dollars.

What is the directory listing worth?

Everyone wants to sell you a directory listing for your law practice. Directories big and small, national, local, and practice area specific promise you a lot of traffic, but what is a directory listing worth? It varies considerably depending on the website.

The salespeople for these directories can be persistent and will speak to you about all of their Internet traffic and how important it is for you to associate with their brand. When I am asked, "What is that listing truly worth?" I have found in directory listing valuation that there is a complete disconnect between what the directory listing costs and what the law firm gets back in return. Usually the pricing disconnect favors the directory and seldom the law firm.

Fortunately, the value of a paid directory listing can be calculated. For purposes of this calculation we will refer to the monthly fee for the paid directory listing as "Directory Listing Cost."

What we talked in an earlier chapter about the challenges of branding for law firms and that holds true for directories too. Brand-association with a major national directory is not likely to do anything for your bottom line, so what we are talking about here is simply the amount of traffic to your website we'll get through the directory listing.

The first question to the salesperson is, "How much traffic will you get through your listing?" The first time you pose this question to the directory's sales representative, that person may tell you a very large number about how many visitors they get per year. This is not a helpful number.

You then ask again for how much traffic will come to the listing that they are trying to sell you. Specifically, ask how many people navigate to the page where your listing will be located, and how many people have clicked over the last 6 months on the listing in the exact place on the page where your law firm will be located.

This will be a real number much smaller than the first number they gave you, but it is a number that you can work with. If they insist that they do not have access to this information, then you should end the call and tell them to call you back when they have that information. Since they are in the business of selling traffic, they have these traffic numbers, whether they want to share them with you or not.

Now that you have a solid number of actual expected visitors to the proposed directory profile page, let's call this number "Actual Visitors."

The next step is to determine what a comparable visitor would cost in Google advertising. A click from Google will cost a certain sum of money varying by the competitiveness of your geographic market and practice areas. If you are already advertising in Google, then this information is available to you. If you are not advertising in Google and are not sure what a click costs, you can set up an account and run a few ads for a short time for the purpose of getting this information or you can contact me at the email address or phone number provided at the beginning of this book. Let's call this dollar amount "Click Cost."

By multiplying the Actual Visitors by Click Cost, you get a number that is higher or lower than the cost of the monthly directory listing. Let's call this dollar amount "Comparable Google Cost."

But the formula does not stop there because a visitor to a directory profile page is not as valuable as a visitor to your website through a Google search. The reason this is true is because when someone types into a Google search box "San Francisco injury lawyer," there is a 100% chance that they are looking for one. However, people can be on a directory for reasons other than actively searching for legal help. For example, they may be there accidentally or looking for your fax number. Secondly, a visitor brought directly to your website through a Google search to a specific page you designate will be a much more valuable visitor than a visitor to a directory profile page one click removed from your website's homepage.

Therefore, an adjustment needs to be made for the difference in the quality and destination of visitors. In this case, I somewhat arbitrarily assign a value adjustment of 1.25 in favor of the Comparable Google Cost.

So now it comes down to this equation:

Comparable Google Cost times 1.25 we'll call your "Adjusted Comparable Google Cost." As for the evaluation of the directory listing, it is simply a matter now of comparing the Directory Listing Cost to this number. If the Directory Listing Cost is cheaper than the Adjusted Comparable Google Cost, then the directory listing is a good value.

To put it more simply, if you multiply the directory traffic by what the same traffic would cost in Google advertising, this will give you an approximate value for the directory listing. Then, if the Google clicks would be the same or cheaper than the traffic from the directory, then you may as well spend that directory money in Google instead.

Very seldom have I found a directory listing worth as much as it costs.

I do want to add that there are other reasons to be in a directory other than traffic. For example, there is a search engine optimization value for some directories (but not all directories). Secondly, if there is negative material about your law firm on the first page of Google's search results, a directory listing for your law firm can help push that negative content further down on the Google search results page.

Other Opportunities for Traffic

There are number of things that you can do in-house, free of charge (except for the law firm's staff time) that can bring more visitors to your firm's website. These activities include maintaining and updating your profiles at free online directories, including Avvo.com, as well as making the most of networking sites like LinkedIn.

Quora

The question and answer forum, Quora, can keep your law firm in front of a large number of people in the Quora community. By responding to inquiries like, "How do I find a good lawyer?" and participating in conversations relating to your practice areas, people will come to know you as an authority on topics that interest you.

You can now advertise in Quora based on specific questions or on broad topics like the following:

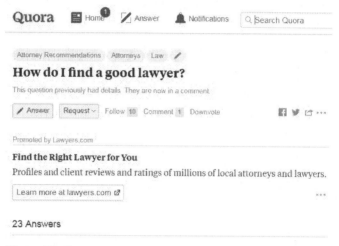

Figure 75. Quora question-and-answer advertising.

I have no experience with Quora but it may be worth exploring. As of this writing, it's new and the topic targeting is limited to the following categories:

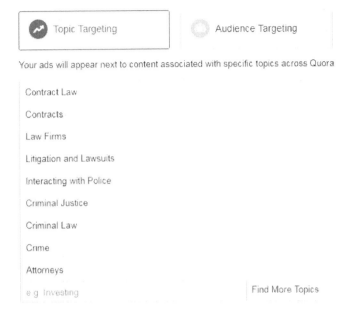

Figure 76. Quora topic advertising.

Avvo

Avvo advertising comes in a few different flavors, including call leads, priority placement in it's search results, and flat fee services. The idea is that you buy into a geographic zone for certain practice areas. Through a dedicated toll-free number, they can monitor time, lengths and originating phone number from your listing.

I have known some lawyers liking it and others quitting, disappointed, after the 90-day trial period.

It isn't cheap and naturally you'd only want to try it if you have a "10.0 Superb" rating. If you're talking to an Avvo sales representative, don't accept their pricing as take-it-or-leave-it because I have seen them offer substantial discounts to close a deal.

Figure 77. The author's 10.0 Superb rating (although he hasn't practiced law in 24 years).

ETHICS ALERT

In addition to advertising your profile to get people to make contact with you, Avvo allows an attorney to sign up to provide legal services for a flat fee. The way it works is that Avvo sets fees for different types of legal services and refers clients seeking those services to participating attorneys. Avvo then charges the attorney a "per service marketing fee."

As of this writing, several states have found this to be an illegal fee-split with a non-lawyer under Rule 5.4. South Carolina, New Jersey, Ohio and Pennsylvania have condemned the practice as an ethics violation and there may be other states that have done so that I'm not aware of.

North Carolina (as always, for better or worse) is the outlier, which as of this writing, is considering a change to their rules to allow the fee-split.

If you're tempted to participate in this Avvo offering, please check to see whether your state has had a chance to condemn it yet, because I predict they will eventually.

Craigslist, Newsletters and Press Releases

Law firms in some communities find that posting regularly in the legal classifieds at craigslist.org can result in some traffic coming to their website from Craigslist users who are seeking legal help.

E-newsletters to your email contacts list can help get people to your website. You should also have a checkbox on your website, possibly connected to your contact form, allowing people to sign up for your newsletter. Whether you're currently publishing a newsletter or not, it never hurts to have the growing list of emails in inventory for future use. We touch briefly on e-newsletters in a later chapter.

Occasional press releases can help bring people to your website. Some press release websites like PRWeb (prweb.com) are favorites of Google and it is a fast and simple way to bury negative content about your law firm if necessary. The cost of a PRWeb press release posting as of now is $149 per press release.

Some lawyers write columns periodically for local newspapers and other community-based online blogs to get their firm's name in front of an audience.

Local Banner Advertising

Local newspaper websites, radio station websites and the like, often offer banner advertising opportunities. The banners give you an opportunity to display your message to a certain group of visitors to the local website at a fixed monthly cost.

There are a lot of things to think about when it comes to banner advertising of this nature, but the main issue, like with any type of advertising, is this: how much is it going to cost and what are you getting? Are there alternatives that deliver more bang for your limited marketing buck?

Each local website and what they are offering is different so it is hard to generalize about whether it is a good use of marketing dollars or not. However, in every case where I have had an opportunity to compare the cost of the banner advertising against other traffic and exposure opportunities, I have recommended against this type of advertising. Here's why:

What we're buying through banner advertising is ad views and click traffic. The value of what we're buying is easiest described in an example.

Let's say that your local news website wants $250 per month and they say they will get your firm's banners in front of 50,000 website visitors per month. Good. We know what they're charging and what we're getting in return for our money.

This has a calculable value which may be more or less than $250 but we're not even going to bother with that. We're just going to compare it to Google "Remarketing" banner advertising.

As we describe elsewhere in this book, Google's "Remarketing" advertising allows us to display ads to local people all over the Internet who fit certain criteria - people who have been to our websites before, and once Google has enough information about our ideal website visitors, people who have been on websites similar to ours and match our visitors' profiles, for example, visitors to other law firms who are also using Remarketing.

In this form of advertising, Google shows your banners at YouTube, Yelp, NY Times and millions of other websites with whom Google has a relationship.

Remarketing banner advertising is cheap and the number of ad displays is amazing. By way of example, I manage the advertising of one advertiser that has over 1 million banner ad displays per month, every ad shown to people physically within their medium-sized metropolitan area. Their clicks cost $0.24 cents a piece and in one typical month, they got 3,584 visitors to their website for a total cost of $835.44.

Now let's take that data back to our example. If we were to throttle this back to $250 per month (because we have complete control over our monthly Google spend) to match the hypothetical cost of the local news site banners, we'd be talking about getting Google to deliver 360,000 ad displays and maybe we'd get 1,075 visitors (results of course will vary a little by community) to our website.

Now that we know what the local news website is selling and what Google can deliver, let's compare what you get for $250/mo (or $100/mo or whatever your actual budget happens to be):

(1) The local news site promises to shows your ads to 50,000 visitors to their news site. For the same money, Google would show your banners to up to 360,000 on many of the largest and most heavily trafficked websites on the web.

(2) The local news site shows your ads to anyone who comes to their website. Google shows your ads only to people in the geographic limits you have set, and only to people who have previously been to your website or who match a profile of people who have visited your websites.

(3) With the news site, they show your banner when they choose to show them and you don't have a great deal of control over placement on the page or the time of day or the location of the viewer.

In Google, you pause your banners when you want, for budgetary or other reasons, set the daily, weekly or monthly schedule when you want to run them, narrow the geographical boundaries or widen them as the whim strikes you, exclude specific websites or entire classes of websites from showing your ads, tell Google you only want your ads to show "above the fold" and a few other interesting refine-able elements.

And you can re-purpose the banners as often as you like. For example, this month we can show 360,000 banners to reach DUI defendants, and next month we instead run a more general criminal law campaign, and the next month to showcase an important event at your law firm.

Here's the bottom line: I can say with a fair amount of certainty that whatever the local news site is offering, unless it's nearly free of charge, would be eclipsed by what you would get from Google banners for the same price - and you'd be getting your ads in front of some very targeted people.

Facebook Local Services

Facebook has launched, very quietly, without any public announcement as of this date, competition for Yelp. A Facebook user can now look for a service and view Facebook business pages with reviews showing up, just like people have been doing for years in Yelp.

You can find it here:

https://www.facebook.com/services/

Despite the fact that it's no a few years old, it's hard to use and requires that a user choose from a pre-defined list of categories to get any results. The list is for now limited and kind of arbitrary. Below are the current choices for "Lawyer" and notice that "Personal Injury Lawyer" is not among the options.

Figure 78. Facebook local service categories.

To view the list of categories, you need to start typing "Lawyer." The list is different if you use the plural "Lawyers." There is no list if you search for

"Attorney" or "Attorneys." It doesn't look like you can search for a specific company yet.

The service directory clearly requires a lot of refinement, which is maybe why they haven't announced it yet. Soon, I'm sure, we'll have more flexible search features and paid top placements like at Yelp.

As it develops, if Facebook users start to use it, then here is what we'll need to do to take advantage of it.

(1) If your law firm doesn't have a Facebook Fan page, please set one up. It's free.

(2) Get some artwork in there and details about your law firm.

(3) Post once in a while if you feel like it and get your staff, friends, relatives and colleagues to "Like" the page.

(4) Then start getting reviews just like you've been doing at Yelp and Google+

It doesn't appear that reviews are a ranking factor in Facebook Services and it's unclear to me at first glance why they favor certain Fan pages over others. We'll know more soon enough.

Facebook Local

Facebook Local, unlike Facebook Local Services, described above, is an app that allows users to find nearby things to do and places to go. So far, it's only for entertainment, with categories like food, drinks, fitness, film, music, etc.

It's worth watching how this app evolves. It may someday include local service providers like lawyers, plumbers and the like, and it probably will soon enough allow us to advertise lawyers there.

Chapter 10. Google Advertising

Google advertising is so important and can be such a productive source of leads that it needs its own chapter to fully describe the amazing marketing opportunities that it presents to the solo practitioner and small law firm. Targeting options like time of day, zip codes, income levels and more, give an attorney unprecedented choices when trying to reach their ideal client types.

In addition, a 2017 report revealed that over the last 2 years, clicks in Google's organic results are down 25% in favor of ads on PCs, and clicks are down 55% in favor of ads on mobile.[28] This means that the value of visibility in Google ads is increasing, while the value of visibility in Google's organic results is diminishing.

Google's offerings can be put into three categories: (1) Search advertising, (2) Display advertising (banners), and (3) YouTube advertising.

Google advertising can bring a lot of targeted traffic to your law firm's website and give you immediate, first page placement for every search term that is important to your law practice. The higher up your ads place in the search results, the more likely your ads will be clicked on by someone searching for legal help in Google. When you can afford it, data from Google shows that it is important to be in the first three ads whenever possible, ideally in the top position so that your ad displays in the first result on mobile phones, and at the very least the fourth spot.

If you were to perform searches in Google for various lawyer-related searches, you will see the firms and directories against which you will be competing for top placement. Some of these law firms and directories that are already advertising may have very large monthly budgets for their Google advertising, probably more than most small law firms can hope to invest. However, with a limited budget, a small law firm can still be extremely competitive against aggressive, well-funded law firms and directories for short periods of time during the week.

Optimal Placement of Your Google Search Ads

What time of day your ads run and where your ads show up in Google's search results page will make a difference in how effective your Google advertising is at getting people to make contact with you. This includes being mindful of where your ads display on mobile devices and how your ads display elsewhere on the web, in the case of Google Display and Remarketing advertising.

Where in Google's search results should your listing or ad be visible?

Recent heatmap studies show that Google users view Google search results in predictable ways. The most heavily viewed and clicked on area of Google search results is the area below the top three ads at the top of Google's index.

The second most heavily viewed area in Google's search results is the top three ads at the top of the page. It's been found that many people perceive these ads as relevant to their search results (although we'll see later that placement in this area is largely a matter of how much a law firm is willing to pay Google when someone clicks on the ad).

For years, the third most viewed area in Google's search results was the map in the upper right-hand corner and the fourth ad just below the map. A study last year showed a large shift in Google user behavior in terms of where they looked at the page after performing a search. With the top part of the page continuing to be the most important part of the search results, Google users now will more often skim the results up and down the page.

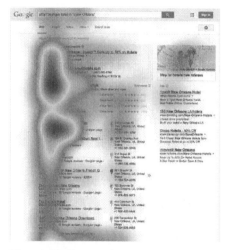

Figure 79. Recent heatmap study showing Google user eye behavior.

Some Google users scroll to the bottom of the first page but very seldom navigate to the second page of Google's search results.

I'm not aware of any heatmap studies for Google's newly designed search results page and how Google users may focus on the page in relation to the four top ads. The click-through rate on the fourth ad position is good which indicates that the ads at the top continue to be an important hotspot, as it is above.

When should you be visible in Google's search results?

In an earlier chapter we looked at overall search activity by day of week and the following figure shows Google search activity for five high-volume law-related searches. In the graph you will see spikes and valleys over several months of data. Each spike in the graph indicates a Monday or Tuesday, and each valley indicates a Sunday. The sharpest Monday/Tuesday spikes shown below are for divorce and criminal law-related searches.

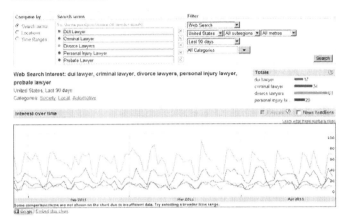

Figure 80. Law-related search volume by day of week for select practice areas.

The next figure shows Google search activity during a typical Monday. This graph shows that the majority of law-related searches takes place between the hours of 9 AM and 4 PM with the heaviest search volume occurring between 9 AM and noon.

While you have little control over when your website is visible in Google's index, you have complete control over when your ads show during the days of the week and time of day.

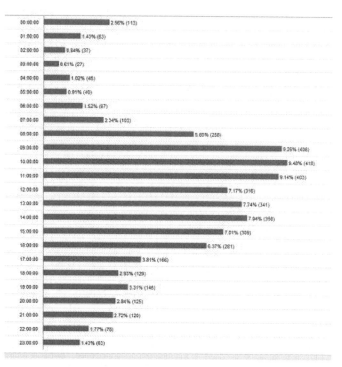

Figure 81. Law-related search volume by hour of day.

In the figures shown above, we saw that most law-related search activity occurs on Mondays and Tuesdays during work hours. As discussed previously, when advertising in Google with a limited budget, it is recommended that you set your ads to run during these days and hours of the week. For example, depending on your market, if you allocate $500 per month to Google advertising, you can place your ads very high on the page during business hours on Mondays. In more rural communities, $500 per month may allow you to run your ads during business hours on some Tuesdays as well. If your law practice is located in a large metropolitan area, then $500 will likely not get you more visibility than maybe several Mondays during the month.

Landing Pages

An important part of Google advertising is creating content to which to link your ads. Practice area pages specific to the phrase you are bidding on have come to be known as "Landing Pages." An example of a Landing Page might be about truck accidents. For the phrase, "truck accident lawyers," and the like, your ads would contain the words, "truck, accidents, lawyers," and those ads would be linked to the truck accident page that you have created for this purpose.

This naturally applies to motorcycle accidents, product liability, medical malpractice, and any other practice areas for which you may be interested in advertising. For family law cases, your Landing Pages may be divorce, custody, support, alimony and the rest.

There are several reasons why Landing Pages are important. First, people are more likely to make contact with you if they are brought to a page that relates very specifically to their legal problem. They will feel like they've found the expert they've been looking for.

The second reason is because Google wants you to have content that relates to the user's search. Google looks at the pages to which your ads are linked and if your ads relate to the topic of the user's search and if the user behaves suitably on your website, like staying on the page for a while, reading your content, and better yet, making contact with you through the content form, Google sees you as a valuable information source and is more likely to show your ads and more likely to discount your cost per click.

The content of your landing pages does not have to be especially substantive in law. In fact, you don't want the pages to read like Wikipedia entries on various legal topics. Instead, you want your entries to be more emotive in content, wherein you make it clear to visitors to the page that you care about their legal problems, that you can help them through this difficult time, and that you have the experience to help them through it.

The typical formula is to begin the page with an emotional appeal to the effect that you know what they are going through. The middle part is about your unique value proposition, and the last part is a call to action: "Contact us for a free, no obligation consultation. We want to help."

Inserting good stock photography, not a scale of justice or gavel, will give some visual interest and hopefully keep the user on the page for more than a few seconds. Streaming a video to that page on the topic of, for example, divorce, and how you can help them with their divorce case, will help people grow comfortable with you before their initial contact.

Core Principles and Mechanics of Google Advertising

There are several important concepts that should be understood before we embark upon a more detailed description of setting up the Google account itself.

Factors that go into where in the page your ads place ("Ad Rank")

It is widely known that Google advertising is in large part an auction: a bidding war with other firms and directories in your community who are trying to reach the same legal consumers. The more you bid, generally speaking, the higher your ad places with the search terms that you're bidding upon (we will discuss bidding fundamentals later in the section of this chapter about the mechanics of setting up your Google account).

But there are several factors that Google takes into account, in addition to the amount of your bid, when it is deciding where to place your ads in the search results. It is important to be mindful of all these factors so that you can get your ads to place in the top three spots as affordably as possible. If you do what Google requires of you as an advertiser, your ads can place higher on a Google search results page even if your bid is lower than some of the other firms on the results page.

Each of these several factors will serve to increase your "Quality Score," which in turn will lower your cost per click for the search phrases that you are bidding on.

Quality Score is a number between one and 10 that Google assigns to each of your search phrases when deciding where to place your ad and how much to charge you for the click. The higher your Quality Score, the lower your cost per click and the higher your ad places in the results. For example, if you are bidding three dollars per click for the phrase "child custody lawyer" and you have a high Quality Score, your cost per click for that phrase may only be $1.90. If your Quality Score for that search phrase is low, you are more likely to pay close to three dollars for that click.

Google's Quality Score formulation is complicated and some of it is unknown to advertisers. The following factors are known to be important in making sure that the Quality Score for all of your search phrases is as high as possible:

"Relevance of the ad text" refers to the content of each of your ads. When one of your ads contains the words that the Google user typed into the Google search box, Google will increase your Quality Score and bold the matching words—which will make your content more visible and more likely to be clicked upon, which serves to improve your "Click through rate.".

"Click through rate" refers to the percentage of people who click on your ads as compared to the number of people who view them. The higher the percentage of people who click through to your website from one of your ads, the higher your Quality Score for that specific search term. Conversely, the lower your click through rate, the lower your Quality Score, and accordingly, the more you will spend for the click.

"Landing Pages" refers to pages on your website that people are brought to when they click on one of your ads. Your Quality Score will be higher if your ads link to content that is very specific to the user's search term. For example, if you are running an ad for the search term "motorcycle accident lawyer," your Quality Score will be higher if that ad links to a page about motorcycle accidents. We will discuss this more below.

"Historical keyword performance" refers to how well your search phrases have performed previously in your account.

Mechanics of setting up a Google advertising account

When advertising in Google, you need to take an expansive approach when it comes to keyword selection and ad writing – lots of ads and lots of keywords.

Some search phrases are obvious, competitive and expensive, whereas other search phrases with lower search volumes are less competitive and cheaper. For example, "car accident lawyer" is high-volume and expensive to bid upon whereas "rear end accident lawyer" is relatively low-volume and less expensive to bid upon.

For a typical personal injury firm, your keyword inventory would include a minimum of few thousand search phrases. Some areas of law like immigration and bankruptcy will often have keyword inventories in the hundreds. Over time, accounts naturally grow as we become aware of different ways that people search. Our oldest and most mature account has been running for 10 years and currently has over 31,000 phrases it its various campaigns.

Negative keywords are important, too. These are keywords that you put into your campaign to tell Google that you never want your ad to show if someone types in the word as part of their search. For example, if you're a criminal defense attorney, you naturally want your ads to show on the search "criminal defense attorney" but not on the search "pro bono criminal defense attorney." By adding "pro bono" as a negative keyword, your ads won't show when someone includes those words in a Google search. When we build a campaign, we include over 9,000 negative keywords to start in order to minimize the number of undesirable clicks. And this list grows within your account as Google apprises us of new, unique search terms to exclude.

When setting up your account, you need to put your phrases into specific groups and attach them to one or more ads that pertain to that specific group of phrases. For example, if you have a group of phrases relating to "divorce lawyers," then you would attach that to an ad that had the words "divorce lawyer" in the body of the ad (which goes to "relevance of the ad text" that was previously discussed).

The challenge here is that if you have an inventory of a few thousand phrases in your account, you'll also need a large inventory of ads - over one thousand ad variations is not unusual. Ad-writing is the heavy lifting of setting up a Google account.

During the setup of your ad groups, you set the bids for the phrases within that ad group and later you determine the settings for the entire campaign; for example, the days and hours you want the ads to run and the amount you want to spend per day.

Then after you put in billing information so that Google can charge you for clicks, you're ready to go.

Managing your Google account

Once your Google account is live, you should login often to monitor its performance. By watching your average position you can determine whether your bids are too high or too low. For example, if your average position is 2.5, that means you are usually[29] in the second or third spot in the top three spots, which is a good place to be.

To be visible on a mobile device you need to be in the top three (sometimes four) spots because that is how many ads Google shows on a hand-held device. The top ad garners by far the most clicks so if your budget will allow it and if you have a version of your website formatted for mobile devices, this placement is important. This means the your average position should be maybe around 1.2 (position 1.0 may indicate that you're bidding too much).

If your average position is 1.1 or 1.2, that means you are usually at the top of the desktop ads and usually visible at the top on mobile devices until your daily budget has been depleted.[30] If you have budget issues, you may even consider lowering your bid to settle into the 1.5 spot[31] or accept that you'll have less up-time than you'd like. If your average position is 6.5, that means that your ad is usually below the scroll bar and is very unlikely to be clicked on, which means you should increase this bid if you can.

In addition to bidding, you will need to pay attention to the Quality Score for your keywords. If your Quality Score is too low for certain phrases, remove them from your account. For example, if a search phrase has a Quality Score of one, that phrase can damage your ad group's and account's historic performance, resulting in an artificially high cost per click.

It is also important that you run variations of your ads within an ad group and compare click through rates so that you can run the ads that Google users are most likely to click on. For example, if your ad group is about "child custody lawyers," then you should have two or more ads connected to those phrases with the words "child custody lawyers" in the body of the ads, speaking to different selling points about your law firm; for example, your firm's years of experience or your cost-effectiveness.

"Conversion tracking" is a tool that Google provides to record how many people make contact with you through your Google advertising. By monitoring your conversions, you can assess whether your website is performing to expectations. As we discuss in other places in this book, a 15% conversion rate is our baseline while a 5% conversion rate strongly suggests that your website is underperforming (or your keywords aren't targeted enough).

Setting up and managing a Google advertising account is complicated, has a steep learning curve, and is constantly changing. A small campaign with a modest budget may be set up and run in-house, but a more expansive account with a larger budget probably should be outsourced so that your average cost per click is kept to a minimum.

Keep your advertising budget in accord with your expected return on investment

It's important to have realistic expectations when it comes to Google advertising. Visibility on Google's first page through its Sponsored Listings means immediate, high-quality traffic to your website. If your account is well-built and closely managed, the advertising will bring in consumers at an advanced stage of the buying process, ready to lawyer-up.

That said, one must consider the investment that it takes to get a client into an attorney's caseload. If 15% of the people who come to your website make contact with you, that's very good. If one in five of those inquiries is something you're interested in, that's good too. If you can jump on that good lead and get them into your office, terrific, you've got a new client through your Google advertising.

But now, how much did you spend in Google advertising to get that client and what does it mean for your return on investment? Keeping in mind that one client from Google advertising isn't going to give you enough data to look at, if you've been advertising for a while and have only 3 or 4 clients, or none, then you can look at what you've brought in to see if you're getting an adequate return on your marketing investment.

Let's say that a DUI client brings in on average $3,500 to your law practice. Let's also say you want to double your investment from advertising. That means that you should plan to spend $1,750 in Google advertising for each paying client you get. Even if you want to triple your return, you would still need to spend $1,167 for each new client.

The bottom line is, if your goal is to get two new clients each week through Google advertising, do the math and budget accordingly. If you're not getting the return that you had hoped, contact me at the phone number or email address I gave in the book's introduction.

There are a number of factors that could be at issue and the matter should be explored to see if there is room for improvement—and there usually is. Some common issues are that the lawyer's expected return is more than can be hoped, or maybe your website isn't doing enough to cause people to make inquiries; or maybe the Google advertising account isn't being as productive as it could be.

Click Fraud

The term "click fraud" refers to the unscrupulous practice of clicking on a competitor's Google ads with the goal of depleting their advertising budget. This is a problem in Google advertising and Google doesn't care.

The following graphic shows a blatant example of click fraud in one of my client's accounts: many searches on obvious, high-volume, expensive search terms, in a short period of time.

If you monitor your search terms report often, you may detect unlikely search patterns that require immediate attention. For fraud protection, I use PPCsecure (http://ppcsecure.com/). It monitors the IP addresses of people who click on your ads and sends you daily reports. I set it up to automatically block IP addresses after they've clicked on one of my clients' ads 3 times.

There may be other comparable software out there, but not from Google. It would be easy for them to create something like PPCsecure, probably in a day, but they have chosen not to.

Search term	Impr. ? ↓
Total	4,542
car accident attorney houston	116
car accident lawyer houston	112
car accident lawyers in houston tx	106
car accident lawyer houston tx	100
car accident lawyer in houston	99
car accident attorneys houston tx	80
car accident attorney houston tx	76
car wreck lawyer houston	74
houston car accident lawyers	69

Figure 82. Example of Google click- fraud.

I have had several heated conversations with Google on this topic because it would be easy enough for Google to have safeguards in place: click fraud is easy to detect and an abuser can be blocked from seeing ads in the future through the IP address.

Should You Consider Outsourcing Your Google Advertising?

If your Google account is going to be built properly and optimally, it requires a lot of work and substantial expertise due to its complexity. It may be tempting to save the setup fee by developing it yourself and investing the money you save on future advertising.

Every company like mine charges a setup fee because it takes a lot of time and know-how. With the typical personal injury account I mentioned earlier, for example, it typically entails over 2,000 phrases and over 1,200 ad variations. Include with that hundreds of unique bids on these ad groups, among multiple campaigns, and that's a lot of work.

Can you do it yourself?

Yes, you can. Go to Google.com/adwords, create an account, and set it up. There's a toll-free number you can call and talk to a representative, who will walk you through it. You won't be talking to someone who will help you set up a very complex campaign. Their primary task is to make sure that you have one campaign set up, containing one ad, at least one phrase and bid, and most importantly, a valid credit card so that Google can charge you for clicks. Beyond that guidance through the setup process, you're mostly on your own.

Is it a good idea to do it yourself?

A lot of money can be squandered on a poorly-built and/or under-managed Google campaign. Here are some common issues I see when I perform audits of other accounts or when I take over an existing account.

(1) KEYWORDS:

I've seen Google campaigns targeting too few keywords, with the advertiser bidding on obvious, expensive keywords like "car accident lawyers" while ignoring cheaper keywords like "car crash law firm."

A typical, mature personal injury Google account should have somewhere between 1,500 and 5,000 keywords, depending on the expansiveness of the advertiser's personal injury practice.

An insufficient number of keywords results in an unnecessarily high average cost-per-click, so you get less traffic than you could for your marketing investment. We need to cast the net as wide as possible and bid on as many of the low volume search phrases as we can.

(2) NEGATIVE KEYWORDS:

A "negative keyword" is a word that you put into your account when you don't want your ad to show for a search that has that specific word in it. A classic negative keyword is "salaries." You want your ads to show for "criminal lawyer" but you don't want them to show for "criminal lawyer salaries." Under-utilization of negatives results in a lot of bad clicks which needlessly squander your marketing dollars.

I find that negative keywords are universally under-utilized. I've seen accounts with a few dozen negatives, some with a few hundred. My campaigns typically have over 9,000 negatives from the start, with the list growing every week.

(3) POOR TARGETING:

If you have a limited marketing budget, you want to run your ads during Google primetime (Mondays and Tuesdays, 9 AM to about 1 PM) and never after hours or weekends (except in rare instances when it makes sense to do so). Targeting certain device types, maybe wealthier suburbs/zip codes, maybe higher level income-level demographics, can result in a higher quality lead.

Making sure that the words "lawyer" or "attorney" (and their plurals) are part of every keyword helps ensure that the searcher is looking for legal help, not just information.

(4) CHANGES AT GOOGLE:

Google is constantly changing, and for the most part improving, but not every change in Google advertising is a good thing. An example from October 2017 was an announcement from Google that you can now expect up to a 100% daily budget over-spend based on daily search volume. That means that you have to very regularly monitor your daily spend or you risk spending twice what you expected to spend in a given month.

Ultimately, what it comes to is how much bang for your marketing buck are you going to get? In the same way that I would hire a lawyer for my personal injury case because I want that huge settlement, you should give serious thought to outsourcing this to a professional because you want to get the best cases for the lowest possible marketing investment.

If you're running a campaign and it's not being run optimally, or you're bringing your paid traffic to a website that isn't performing well, or you're paying too much for your clicks, or a combination of these, in the end you're throwing away money. The management fees that you'd be paying to a competent provider would be cheaper than the money that's being wasted in underproductive advertising and overpriced clicks.

Chapter 11. Search Engine Optimization

Search Engine Optimization (SEO) Overview

SEO refers to things you do to your website and elsewhere on the Internet to make your website appear more relevant for certain search phrases to Google (and the other lower volume search engines). The long-term goal is to get your website to place on the first page of Google's search results and to get the website to stay there for as long as you can.

The SEO process can take months and should be started as soon as possible.

Google reportedly considers 200+ different factors when determining the relevancy of a website for a specific search query and most of these factors are unknown to everyone except for a group of scientists at Google. In a rare moment of candor, in March 2016, Google disclosed that the top two ranking factors were links and content, ending a lot of speculation and disagreement among SEO professionals.

With the otherwise limited amount of information at our disposal, and a lot of speculation and trial and error behind us, what follows is a general description of the SEO process as a lot of SEO companies do it.

The four main steps in SEO are very generally (1) research to select your target phrases, (2) working your target phrases into your website, (3) creating content about your target phrases, and (4) building links.

Selecting your target phrases

The first step in SEO is to figure out your "keywords" or more descriptively, "target phrases" - the search phrases you want to target that are realistic to target. The target phrase is a search term that is very specific to your law practice, for example, "New York personal injury lawyer" or "Albany family law attorneys."

When deciding what phrases you want to target for your SEO effort, your criteria should be 3-fold: (1) you should naturally select phrases that are important to your law practice, (2) the phrases should have enough search volume to make the effort worth your trouble, and (3) you should make sure that the competition for your desired search phrases isn't so extreme that the effort is futile.

For example, if a law firm wanted to target "New York malpractice lawyer," they may find in their research that the search volume is high but that the phrase is so competitive that the law firm could work for years and its website still won't overtake the larger firms and legal directories that dominate the first page of Google's search results. In that same law firm's research, they may find that "New York birth injuries lawyer" has less search volume but a higher likelihood of successful first page placement and the law firm may go with that phrase instead.

Google makes competition and search volume reports available to Google advertisers but SEO companies who want your business can run these reports for you as well (sometimes free of charge).

Working your target phrases into your website

The work you do on your website to improve your Google ranking is called "on-page SEO." On-Page SEO is a process whereby you work your target phrases into the content and meta tags of your site so that Google sees you as relevant to users searching for your target phrases.

When integrating your phrases into your website, you should keep in mind that you are first and foremost writing for people who come to your website, not Google – excessive keyword stuffing can drive people away, defeating the point of increasing your website traffic. Plan to have one or more pages and/or blog posts on your website for the case types that are most important to your law practice.

Let's say you're a family lawyer in Albany and you've selected 2 or 3 phrases for which you'd like to show up in Google's results (e.g., "Albany divorce lawyer" or "divorce attorneys in Albany"). In the course of your on-page SEO then, you'd emphasize these phrases as often as possible on your divorce practice area page and elsewhere on your website, without damaging the professionalism of the content by having your phrases in there too often.

One of Google's more important ranking factors is the "title tag" of each of your website's pages. The title tag goes into the source code of your website and goes between <title> and </title> at the top of your page. Put your most important target phrases first, including your geographic qualifier (like "Albany"). Try to limit the length of your title to 70 characters.

The headings in your content are very important, with the highest level heading (your <H1> headings) naturally being the most important.

Hyperlinks between the pages on your website will help Google crawl through it. By having good keyword phrases within the text of the links, Google will better understand the subject matter of the pages to which the links connect.

For example, let's say there's a link on your website which reads "Click here to learn more about our experienced Albany divorce lawyers" bringing people to your "About Us" page. If you have the hyperlink on the whole sentence or just the 'click here' portion, that doesn't tell Google exactly what is being linked to and is a wasted opportunity to emphasize to Google some important phrases. Better would be to have the hyperlink on the words "experienced Albany divorce lawyers", so that Google knows what the page to which you're linking is about.

Creating content

The mantra is "Content is King" because Google has made it clear that it wants your website to be rich in good content—content that people will read and share. You create content by writing more specific practice area pages; for example, by sub-dividing your vehicle accident page into several pages on the topics of car accidents, motorcycle accidents, and so on.

You also should regularly blog on topics relating to the target phrases that you selected in the first stage of the SEO process described previously. If your content is good and keyword-rich, Google should reward you for the effort.

"Social signals" like when a visitor to your website "tweets" about one of your blog posts, comments upon your blog post, or links to a page on your website from a social bookmarking site all indicate that people like your content, making it worthy of higher placement in Google's search results.

The reality is that law-related content is seldom shared or talked about because it doesn't have the same level of popular interest that topics like celebrity gossip, funny videos, or sporting events do. Consequently, social signals for law firm websites and blogs need to be, to some extent, artificially created.

Building links

The third part of SEO is referred to as "off-page SEO" because it involves things that you do elsewhere on the web to convince Google that you're an important information resource for certain searches. This is simply the deliberate process of gathering links gradually from other websites to your own.

Fundamental to Google's ranking algorithm is the notion that the more websites that link to your website, the more important your website is as an information resource on the web. When Google perceives you as important for a particular phrase, it will typically place you higher in its index.

How do you get other websites to link to your website?

You can get links to your website in a variety of ways. You can list your website on directories, exchange links with colleagues with whom you are not in direct competition, post to guest blogs, set up accounts in social media sites like Twitter and Facebook, participate in networking sites like LinkedIn, and publish content to press release and article sites. The more high quality sites that link to yours, the more Google will think that your site is growing in popularity and importance.

Google My Business and directories

There are companies that send unsolicited emails to your spam folder offering to claim and verify your Google Maps ("Google My Business") listing for a small sum of money but it is recommended that you ignore these solicitations. It is easy to complete your Google My Business page and you are urged to do this in-house.

For Google local results, you need to be visible in a variety of directory types. Some directories are more important than others and you should focus on the directories with the highest "domain authority."

Directories fall generally within three categories: national directories like YP.com, legal directories like Lawyers.com, and local directories, like your community's Chamber of Commerce website.

You should add yourself to as many of these directories as you can, using a local area code for your office phone number and an absolutely consistent name, address and phone number convention ("NAP").

There are companies like Yext that will automate the directory submission process to many national directories for a monthly fee and annual commitment. I normally recommend against using Yext or any of its resellers because the monthly fee, for what is essentially a one-time submission in the first few days of the year-long contract, never made any sense to me. Others may find value in it.

Searches on "best" and other superlatives.

Google reports that searches containing the word "best" (for example, "best criminal lawyers") have increased 80% in the last two years and Google started doing an interesting thing in the summer of 2017:

When people perform a search for "lawyers" in Google, they get maps results based on that search, naturally. But, when they add a superlative like "best lawyers," (or other similar superlatives like "good" or "excellent"), Google serves up different results based on who Google has decided is best in the searcher's community.

Notice below that in a search for "Akron lawyers," the Akron Bar comes up first in the Maps result:

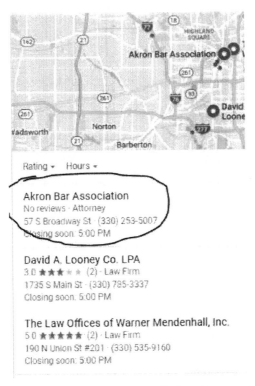

Figure 83. Maps results for "Akron lawyers."

Now notice on the search "best Akron lawyers," the Akron Bar doesn't show in the maps:

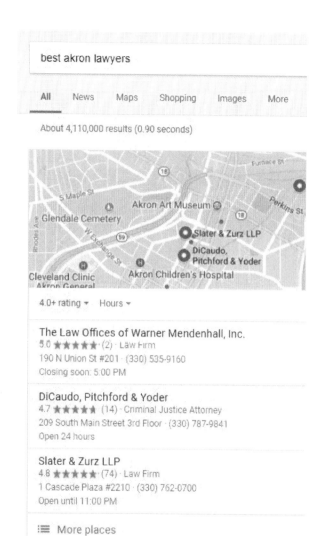

Figure 84. Maps results for "best Akron lawyers."

The difference? Apparently the presence of 5-star Google+ reviews.

Fortunately, Google+ reviews are easy to get because Google doesn't have the same aggressive filtering that

Yelp uses. From what I've seen, every review sticks. In addition, someone doesn't need to actually write a review - someone can simply click on the 5-stars and leave it at that.

Should You Consider Outsourcing Your SEO?

Probably you should. First, SEO is labor intensive and time consuming, and if you'd rather practice law than spend hours modifying your pages and bargaining for in-bound links, you should strongly consider outsourcing the project to a competent SEO company.

Second, your SEO efforts won't help your website overnight. It may be months before you start noticing real gains in terms of ranking on Google's organic search results and increased traffic to your website.

Third, this is an on-going process that you should plan to keep doing for as long as you want to stay high up in Google's search results. This takes time and stamina.

There are software solutions if your website is on WordPress. Plug-ins like Yoast do all of the on-page search engine optimization thinking for you and your SEO provider is probably already using it when working on your site.

Doing your due diligence if you plan to outsource SEO

SEO is very hard work and requires a certain personality type to do it well for the months that it may take to get results. You are strongly encouraged to outsource your SEO to a competent provider.

When you first start talking to an SEO provider, they may start talking about getting your website to rank high in Google's search results. The important question, however, is for what searches your website will rank high. Anyone can get your website to rank high for the name of your law firm but can they get your website to rank high for high-volume searches like "malpractice lawyers" or "divorce attorneys"?

Ask them about their techniques. If they use a lot of buzz words like "structured citations" and "domain authority," get them to explain thoroughly what each term means.

Get references from the prospective SEO provider (especially law-related references) and ask them to provide a list of phrases and websites that they have successfully gotten to the first page of Google's search results. With this list of phrases, perform the searches yourself to see how they did.

Long-tail searches[32]

Some SEO providers will steer you towards the selection of search phrases that are seldom used in Google—after all, it's easier to get you to Google's first page if there's no competition for rankings. You'll want to steer them away from "long-tail searches" because those are not the phrases your SEO professional should be targeting. You will hear from them that Google favors the long-tail search, and that may be true, but there are going to be few of such searches, thus resulting in very little traffic.

The long-tail phrases should be part of your Google advertising, not your SEO. If people seldom search on the phrases, your ads will display as seldom, and it won't cost very much to be visible for those searches. In contrast, high-volume phrases are normally the most competitive in advertising and the most expensive, so the higher-volume phrases should be the focus of your SEO.

It is recommended that prior to hiring an SEO provider, you have them provide you with preliminary search volume estimates for phrases pertaining to your practice areas, as well as your website's current rankings for those phrases in Google's index.

Want to Do Your SEO In-house?

Then go to Appendix A – A Quick Guide to SEO, roll up your sleeves and let's get busy.

Chapter 12. Yelp, Google+ and Online Reviews

This chapter deals with online reviews, positive and negative, and the impact the reviews have on your Ecosystem. It also covers what you can do to get more positive reviews in Yelp and how to minimize the impact of negative reviews.

Why Positive Reviews Are Important

It has become very important for lawyers to have a number of positive reviews. There are two main reasons for this.

First, there appears to be a correlation between positive reviews and how a website ranks in Google's Map results, particularly reviews in Google+, especially as it relates to searches containing superlatives like "best criminal lawyers," as we discuss more in the SEO chapter of this book.

Second, in a study released in 2017,[33] it was found that 85% of consumers say that they trust online reviews as much as they trust personal recommendations.

Ninety percent of consumers say that buying decisions are influenced by online reviews. One 2015 study found that app downloads increased by 340% when the app's rating increased by one star.[34] Conversely, bad online reviews can have a very negative impact on your online presence, again because most people believe and trust reviews.

The Harvard Business Review found that a 1-star difference in ratings resulted in a 5-9% change in revenue.[35]

Positive reviews can help get more people to make contact with you. Of the review sites, the most popular and trusted is Yelp[36] among people who are searching for lawyers.

In an earlier chapter, we discuss why Yelp is an important part of online lead generation. To recap, there are three main reasons why Yelp is important:

First, it's a supporting element to your website because people may go there after visiting your website to research what clients have said about you or find your website through it.

Second, as of this writing, Yelp has been occupying top spots in Google's search results, sometimes before a lawyer's actual website, so people searching in Google may go to your Yelp profile before going to your website.

Yelp User Behavior and Expectations

If a Yelp user likes your reviews, it was found that 72% of the Yelp users would visit your website or call you.

How many positive reviews do you need?

Sixty-seven percent think that 4 to 6 positive reviews are enough and that 85% of Yelp users are satisfied with 7 to 10 positive reviews.

How many "stars" do you need?

Yelp employs a 5-star review system with 5 stars being the highest possible rating and 1 star the lowest. When there is a mix of reviews with different star ratings, Yelp averages the reviews to give you a fractional star rating like 4.5 stars.[37]

Seventy-two percent of Yelp users have been found to think that 2 stars is too low of a rating and of course, the closer your overall rating is to 5 stars, the more Yelp users will be inclined to visit your website or call you.

Taking Control of Your Listing

If you find that you already have a listing, you need to claim it to take ownership of it. Look for your business in Yelp and if you find a listing for your business, you should take control.

Often I am asked why someone would have a Yelp listing if they never set one up for their law firm. The reason is because anyone can set up a Yelp profile of your business for the purpose of leaving a review.

You start the claiming process at Yelp's Business Listings URL, which is biz.yelp.com. Once you are there, type in the name of your business. Yelp will display all of the listings that match your search.

You will notice to the right of each listing that Yelp will display either "Already claimed" or a red button that says "Claim this business," as shown below.

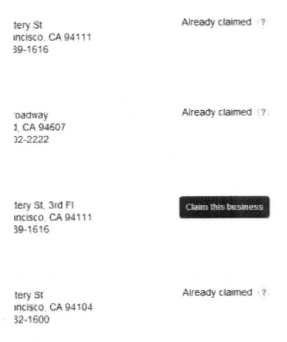

Figure 85. Claiming your Yelp business listing.

Once you have claimed your business listing, you will have some control over the listing's look and messaging. Add some photos and information about your firm.

Figure 86. Your claimed Yelp listing.

Email alerts

Sign up for email alerts so that you are notified whenever you receive a positive or negative review. This will give you an opportunity to thank people for positive reviews and to make repair attempts with those who leave negative reviews.

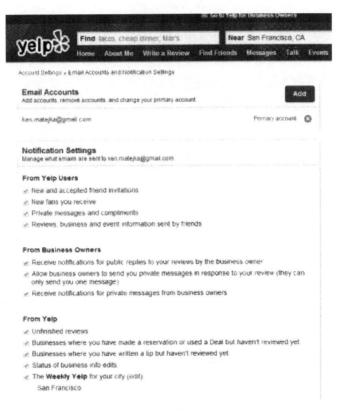

Figure 87. Setting up Yelp email alerts.

What if you have more than one listing on Yelp?

If you have more than one listing on Yelp, it's a good idea to combine them. The way to accomplish this is to claim each of your listings and notify Yelp that a listing is a duplicate.

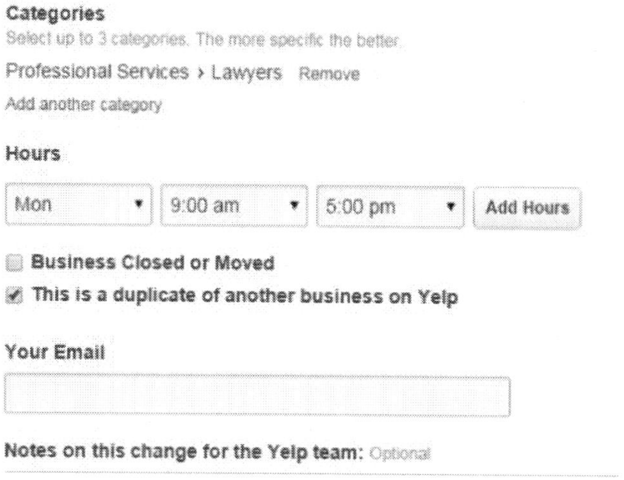

Figure 88. Combining duplicate listings in Yelp.

What if you have no listing at all on Yelp?

If you do not find your business listing in Yelp, you can add your business by creating a new business account at biz.yelp.com.

Add Your Business

Add information about your business below. Yelp reviews each submission, which may take a few days. If your listing is approved, you will be able to create an account on Yelp for Business Owners.

Country

United States ▾

Business Name

Matejka Marketing

Address 1

77 Van Ness Avenue

Address 2

Suite 101

City   **State**   **ZIP**

San Francisco   CA   94102

Phone

(415) 513-8736

Web Address

http://matejkamarketing.com/

Hours

Mon ▾   9:00 am ▾   5:00 pm ▾   Add Hours

Categories

Professional Se ▾   Marketing ▾   Remove

Add another category

Figure 89. Adding your business to Yelp.

What to Do with Negative Reviews

No matter how hard you try, eventually a client is going to be disappointed enough with an interaction or case result to voice it on a review site like Yelp.

A bad review that ranks high in search engine results is going to have a negative impact on your online success. Therefore, you need to do everything you can to minimize the potential damage.

The following is what is possible to do in the eventuality of this happening to you.

Challenge the review

Whether the review is at Yelp or on some other review site, if the review is libelous, you can write to the editors to have it removed.

You may find a review where you do not recognize the author or the circumstances he or she is describing, leading you to a conclusion that it may have been posted by a competitor or by someone who is mistaking you for someone else.

You may recognize the client, but the review is filled with mischaracterizations, falsehoods and vilifying opinions. If you recognize the person and they are expressing their constitutionally protected opinions, then there's not a lot you can do to get Yelp to remove it. Yelp specifically won't get involved in a "he-said-she-said" argument.

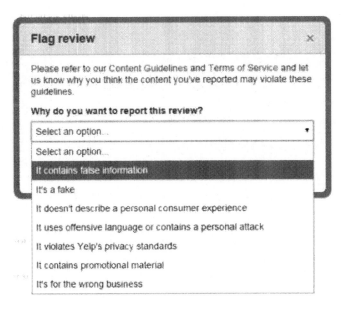

Figure 90. Challenging a Yelp review.

If you would like to have a review taken down, you can write to the editors through a contact form on the website for this specific purpose. When you write, you will make your strongest case for why the review should be removed.

If a few weeks later the review is still there, you may want to follow up with another email requesting that the review be taken down.

Respond to the client

If you know the person who put the review on the website, you may want to respond to the reviewer to see if there is anything that can be done to make things better.

In the case of Yelp, you have an opportunity to reply privately through the Yelp website itself to see if there is any hope of improving the reviewer's attitude toward your lawyer referral program.

If you tried this and it was unsuccessful or if you think it would be pointless to try, you may want to post a public reply if the review site allows.

Posting a public reply

Yelp and some other review websites will give you an opportunity to give your side of the story in the form of a public reply. This can be effective if handled artfully but can be risky if the reviewer wants to post a reply to your public reply, in which case you may be making matters worse.

Bury the review

By eliciting positive reviews from other satisfied clients, you may be able to drive the negative review deeper into your listing and dilute the overall negative impact of the bad rating for your law firm.

Simply asking for reviews from former satisfied clients and giving the link to your Yelp listing (where your negative review exists) may be enough. Plan for many of your reviews, if at Yelp, to be filtered out, but some of them will stick.

Do not post contrived reviews at Yelp or at Google+ because they can often detect that and penalize you for it. Besides, posting fake reviews will run afoul of your State's "false or misleading" communication prohibition of Rule of Professional Conduct 7.1 (RPC 1-400 in California).

Bury the search result

If none of the above has helped and the negative review is still showing prominently in the search results for your firm's name, the next best thing would be to bury the search result by crowding it off the first page of Google's search results with more positive information about you.

Your active social media platforms can be effective by appearing earlier in the search results for your name than a Yelp listing. In addition, posting frequently to your Google+ account should cause that account to rank well in Google's search results.

Google has an apparent fondness for certain press release websites like PRWeb. By putting up press releases at websites like these (often for a small fee - PRWeb as of this writing charges $149 per press release), you should be able to get your handcrafted positive content to rank well.

YouTube can also be helpful in displacing a negative search result.

If you find yourself in this situation, and most law firms will eventually, be proactive in minimizing the negative impact on your law practice. We discuss this issue in more detail in a later chapter about reputation management.

Getting Positive Reviews

There are ways of dealing with negative reviews that are addressed in the previous section, and you should certainly deal with negative reviews first if you have any. Presently, we are going to focus on getting positive reviews.

Yelp's filters

Unfortunately, it's not enough to get positive reviews. You must get positive reviews that do not get "filtered." A filtered review will neither show in your business listing nor will the rating that the reviewer gave you be part of the calculation towards your overall rating.

A lot of positive reviews in Yelp get filtered out because Yelp questions their authenticity. While this is effective in minimizing the number of artificial reviews posted, unfortunately, it screens out many genuine reviews.

If someone joins Yelp, leaves one review, then never reviews again, Yelp is likely to filter that out as questionable. A review from someone who already has an established history of reviewing local businesses is more likely to write a review that sticks.

Here's how you find out who among your former satisfied clients is already an established Yelp reviewer.

First, create a Yelp individual account as a reviewer, and let Yelp scan your email contacts.

Google

www.yelp.com is requesting permission to:

▸ Manage your contacts

Allow access   No thanks

Figure 91. Allowing Yelp to scan your email contacts.

This will give you a list of people who are already Yelp reviewers. Find the established Yelp reviewers whom you served well and where you are sure they would leave a positive review for you.

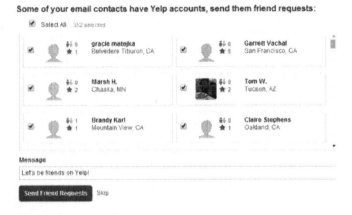

Figure 92. Your email contacts who are already Yelp reviewers.

Next, reach out to the clients[38] who you believe will give you 5-star reviews.[39]

Third, send these email contacts the link to your listing so that it's easy for them to click on it and leave a review.

Keep in mind that you should do this very gradually. Aim for maybe one or two additional 5-star reviews per month. Too many, too fast may be viewed as suspect by Yelp. As of late 2017, Yelp has been cracking down on deliberate review solicitation, threatening to demote the listing in Yelp search results.

Hello,

You are putting your clients' online reputation at risk by soliciting Yelp reviews on their behalf.

Beginning this month we are contacting local businesses that solicit reviews on Yelp to highlight that asking for reviews violates our policies. We explain that engaging in this practice may result in demotion in Yelp search results.

Soliciting reviews for your clients is an illicit tactic that biases their online reputations and search rankings, thus harming consumers, other businesses, and the overall review ecosystem.

For more information on Yelp's stance against review solicitation, see our blog post.

The Yelp Support Team

Figure 93. Yelp's review solicitation warning.

One final note - make sure the reviews are genuine, from actual satisfied clients. Besides the obvious requirements of the Rules of Professional Conduct, Yelp sometimes posts alarming alerts when it uncovers evidence of review fraud. These show up directly in the reviews section with a "Show me the evidence" button.

Figure 94. Yelp's review fraud consumer alert.

Automated Review Gathering

It's not uncommon these days for law firms to send emails to former clients requesting feedback about their services. When done correctly, it's a good practice. It gives the client the feeling that we care about their experience with us, and it also helps us elicit a positive review on Yelp or Google+.

There are automated solutions to get positive reviews from these feedback surveys that are employed by reputation management companies and can also be done in-house.

Here is an example used by one reputation management company that your law firm could implement in-house without much effort or expense.

First, you would send an email to every client for whom you have an email address, with this one question:

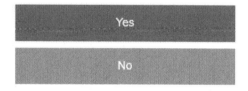

Would you recommend us?

Thank you for your business!
Would you recommend us to your family and friends?

Yes

No

Figure 95. Feedback elicitation email.

If the recipient responds, their choices are "Yes" or "No." If the recipient clicks on "Yes," then they are taken to the law firm's Google+ page to leave a review (hopefully 5 stars) or to your Yelp profile:

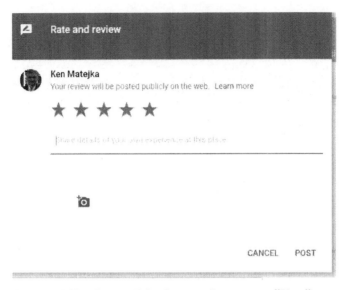

Figure 96. Feedback elicitation email, response "Yes."

If the recipient responds "No," then they are brought to a different page like this:

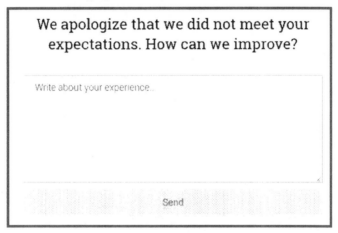

Figure 97. Feedback elicitation email, response "No."

This simple process can bring satisfied clients to your review sites and dissatisfied clients to a location that is not public where they can vent.

Chapter 13. Reputation Management

If there's nothing negative about your law firm online yet, brace yourself for the eventuality. Regardless of how good you are and how hard you work on a particular case, sooner or later, the outcome of one of your clients' case may fall short of their expectations and they'll be disappointed enough to say it publicly. Sometimes a disgruntled former employee or malicious competitor may anonymously post negative content about your firm.

First impressions matter most, so when a Google user is searching for you by name, we should think of page 1 of Google's search results as your public persona. As such, we need to manage as much as possible, the information that shows up in Google so that when people perform a search on our names, they're viewing positive information about us.

There are a number of companies offering "reputation management" services. The services can be expensive and their salespeople can be persuasive when describing how important their services are for you. Sometimes the services are needed and perhaps worth the investment. In other cases, the services are unnecessary or overpriced because there may be a small amount of work to be done that you can do in-house.

For example, I once came upon a law firm that had retained a reputation management company for just a few bad reviews that could be taken care of by the law firm itself with a little training, making it a wasteful use of the law firm's marketing budget.

Below, we're going into what reputation management is, what those companies do for all of that money, and whether this is a service you need.

What is "Reputation Management"?

Reputation management is the process of dealing proactively, in one way or another, with negative online content about you and your law firm that people may find when searching for you by name. Anything online that casts you or your law firm in a negative light, affects your "reputation" and must be "managed."

The negative content one might find about you can come in different forms:

- A bad review on a site like Yelp,
- A critical post to social media,
- A review on RipOffReport.com, or some similar website that encourages negative consumer content,
- A "hate site,"
- Public discipline from your local licensing authority,

- Unflattering press coverage,
- etc.

What does a reputation management company do?

The services provided by a competent reputation management company depends on the type of negative content that exists about you or your firm.

Social media

Your reputation management company should constantly monitor social media for posts about your law firm to ensure that all posts, positive and negative, receive an appropriate, empathetic response from your business.

Review sites

The reputation management company may challenge fake or defamatory reviews on review sites like Yelp and Google+ with the review site editors, while hustling for new, 5-star reviews to dilute the impact of the negative reviews. We cover some of this in the earlier chapter about Yelp.

Hate sites

A "hate site" is a website created by someone who dislikes you enough to go through the trouble to create a website containing lots of negative content about you or your law firm. Often websites about identifiable people rank well in Google for searches on their names.

When the creator of the website can be identified, then a good reputation management company would help you take appropriate actions to get the author to take it down. If the author is unknown, then your reputation manager may retain an investigator to find them.

Sometimes it's impossible to identify the publisher of a hate site. In this instance, your reputation management company would make an effort to crowd it off of Google's first page by creating higher-ranking, more positive content about you.

Consumer complaint sites

Although there are several sites in this category, we'll focus on  Ripoff Report because it is the most famous of them and it tends to rank well in Google's search results.

Ripoff Report is a problem from a reputation management perspective because they have no review filtering or review process for content that's posted on the website. This failing allows any unhappy ex-employee, competitor, or crazy person to go in there and write anything they want about you.

Additionally, for the most part, there is no way to get Ripoff Report to remove a post. They are consistent on this point, citing the value of free speech and what not. They have an expensive "VIP Arbitration" service but if you pay for it, there's no guarantee you'd prevail.

Appealing to the author directly is always an option, but it can back-fire if the person chooses to update their Ripoff Report post with more content. This may make the review even worse and may cause the post to rank even higher in Google's search results.

With a court order, you can get Google to remove the Ripoff Report link from its index entirely, but it's been found that sometimes Ripoff Report will change the link address, causing the post to return to Google's search results.

As with hate sites, sometimes the only remedy is for your reputation management company to bury it in Google's search results so that it no longer appears on page 1.

Negative media and other public information

If you have a criminal conviction, discipline history from your attorney licensing authority or negative press, there's no hope of appealing to the publisher to have it removed. In this case, your reputation management company would work to push that content off of Google's first page with more positive content under your control.

While creating the content, your reputation management company will optimize the content for searches on your name, and variations thereof, to try to get it to out-rank the other negative content.

Do you need a reputation management company?

Reputation management services can be pricy. When they need to bury public information in Google's search results that cannot be otherwise removed, they have to create lots of content about you, build websites, optimize those websites, publish press releases, and all of the other things that would go into saturating Google's first-page search results with links to positive information.

Whether you need a reputation management company depends on the nature, extent and visibility of the negative information about you in Google. If we're simply talking about a few bad reviews on Yelp, Google+ or some other review site, then no, you probably don't need to hire an expensive reputation company. If there is public information of a nature more substantial than just a review, then you might.

So let's see what's out there.

In decided whether you need reputation management services, Google yourself in every possible way someone may search for you (for example, in my case, I'd search for Ken Matejka, Kenneth Matejka, Kenneth F. Matejka, Ken Matejka Attorney, and maybe a few other variations).

Focusing primarily on Google's first page, see what's out there about you that you'd prefer potential clients not see.

If it's just a 1-star Yelp review, you do not need a reputation management company to fix this issue. It's easy enough to get more positive reviews yourself.

In the case of a hate site, a threatening cease-and-desist email may make that content disappear. If the creator refuses, or if you can't figure out who the creator of the site is, then maybe you'll need additional help.

If there's an easily-found public discipline report, criminal record or negative press, then you probably will need outside help to bury it with new material about you.

Due diligence and monitoring results

If you need to a reputation management company would be of benefit, as part of your due diligence, as for success stories and perform the searches yourself to make sure that they have been able to deliver for others in your situation. Ask about their processes and expected timeline.

Once you hire, or if you have already hired, a reputation management company, you may be paying a lot for their services so insist upon detailed breakdowns of their monthly activity and monitor their progress by performing searches for yourself often.

Chapter 14. Cultivating Your Referral Network

Taking Advantage of Online Networking Opportunities

While your website will be a growing source of clients as your Ecosystem's development continues, a productive source of clients for lawyers should also be its referral network of other legal professionals, agencies and organizations in the community.

For decades and still, a lot of networking takes place at events, CLEs, fundraisers, awards dinners, etc. and is in the form of friendly conversations and the exchange of business cards.

If you are a diligent networker, maybe you will send a follow-up email to someone you met at an event, mention again your firm as a trusted place to refer cases they can't handle personally, and add their email address to your e-newsletter subscriber list.

They have your business card too and when they get your email, they will probably remember your conversation, remembering you as a friendly person. But business cards get lost, discarded, or put in a drawer and forgotten about. Soon the recipient's memory of your conversation at that mixer fades away. Then when a client who needs legal help in your practice area contacts that attorney, you're not among the lawyers who come to mind.

The many networking opportunities on the Internet can fix that, keeping your firm's name in the forefront of the minds of other legal professionals and entities when that next referral comes along. Here's how it works:

Let's say at the next event where you mix with other legal professionals, over the course of the evening you exchange business cards with four attorneys and a court clerk, and have short conversations with them about their health, families and work. Write on the back of the business card a few notes of what you talked about so that you can reference those details later. Don't worry about giving out your business cards - the important thing is to get as many business cards from others that you can. Everyone will hand one over if you ask.

The next day you have the five business cards and rather than sliding them into your top drawer and forgetting about them, you send the "Nice meeting you" email referenced above. Then at the same time, you go to each of their five LinkedIn profiles and make a "Connection" request with a personal message, such as "Great meeting you last night. It sounds like you have your hands full with those [kids/dogs/trials/etc,]" They get your email, and they get a second email from LinkedIn telling them that you made a connection request.

Remembering your friendly conversation last night, they go into LinkedIn and accept your connection.

Now, a few weeks later, you "Endorse" them in LinkedIn for one of their practice areas. They get an email that you have endorsed them. They remember you as the nice colleague they met at the mixer - a professional contact that may be useful someday.

Then, maybe three weeks after that, you Follow their Twitter account. They get an email that you just followed them. Ten days later you re-tweet one of their tweets and they get an email from Twitter that you re-tweeted one of their tweets. They are really remembering you now and starting to like you for all of the positive attention.

Then at seemingly random, but pre-calendared, intervals of maybe 6 or 7 weeks, you "Like" their Facebook Fan Page, and then "Like" one or two of their Facebook posts. Then "Favorite" one of their tweets. Later you add them to your Google+ Circles and give them a "Peer Endorsement" at Avvo.com. Then you endorse them for something else in LinkedIn and re-tweet another one of their tweets and "Like" another one of their Facebook posts. And so on.

And they may also have Google+ business pages and LinkedIn Company Pages to follow.

> CAUTION: don't do this too often because it can be perceived as creepy if overdone.

It's worth noting that each time you do something like this, it results in an email to the legal professional to whom you are reaching out. By spacing these activities out over the course of the year, what began as a simple exchange of business cards at a mixer is now a referral source set in cement because that person remembers you and likes you.

Chapter 15. Putting It in Action

OK, now it is time to get started with your online lead generation project. We are going to go through the implementation of the development of your online lead generation system, step-by-step.

Get Your Website Ready

The first part of developing your lead generation system is to lay the foundation, i.e., your website. This is a critical step because once people come to your site, they are going to decide whether to contact you based on how they respond to what they see there.

There is a side issue with your law firm's website, namely, whether you have enough control among other stakeholders at the firm to make changes to the site. If you do, we're golden. If not, try to get the buy-in you need to make the website as productive as you can.

Get a website if you don't have one

The first step for lawyers who don't have websites yet is to get one. If you already have a website, then skip ahead to the next part.

Everything depends on having the right website in place. As discussed previously in earlier chapters that a great website will bring in many more inquiries than a bad website, which will make your online lead generation system as productive as possible.

If you don't have a lot to invest, there are a lot of affordable options for lawyers looking for websites.

Template factories

Template factories produced by major attorney marketing companies will rent a website to you with attractive-sounding add-ons like a listing in their directory. However, when you add up all of the monthly fees paid out over the term of your contract, you'll find a rental from them is quite expensive. Then at the end of your contract, you still don't own a website.

Regardless of what their high-pressure salespeople tell you, just like with a car, it's better to own than to rent.

Custom websites

A custom website from a specialized attorney website company like mine is always an option.

In the industry generally, you can expect a custom website to cost between $5,000 and $10,000 and possibly more, depending on the size of your firm (and the size of your budget, which for some website companies, I believe to be a pricing factor). Our company currently charges $3,750 one-time fee for most attorney websites when bundled with other marketing services. Lots of content migration and special features can add a little to this price but not often and not much.

When selecting a vendor for website development, ask to see their portfolio. If you see gavels and scales of justice in their portfolios, move on to other vendors. Get performance data for websites in their portfolio. A lot of website developers can build beautiful, artsy websites, but don't overly concern themselves about whether legal consumers will respond positively towards it.

For the more budget conscious, there are do-it-yourself options too.

Do-It-Yourself (DIY) websites

Self-help web-building tools can get an inexpensive website up for you in no time and they host the website for you for a low monthly cost. Here are a few more popular DIY website companies.

Wix.com

I built the following website at Wix.com. The homepage seen here took me a few hours and is based on one of their templates. I used a stock photograph that I bought in advance.

Figure 98. Website from Wix.com.

One serious drawback on Wix.com is that it's impossible to embed code into the website, thus making certain types of advertising impossible. When I learned this in their support forum, I stopped working on this website.

I recommend against Wix but it is cheap enough, currently priced at $9.95 per month including hosting.

Squarespace.com

Squarepsace.com is another free website builder with some beautiful and easy-to-use templates. The following figure is an example of a Squarespace website that I built. I found the interface to be intuitive enough to get the homepage together in an afternoon.

Figure 99. Website from Squarespace.com.

Squarespace is my favorite of the do-it-yourself websites. I like it mostly because of a widget for the mobile version of the website that makes it easy to insert a prominent click-to-call feature. It is currently priced at $192 per year, including hosting.

Vistaprint

The company that has been printing your business cards, Vistaprint, is also in the website business. The website in the next figure I created in about 3 hours and most of the time was spent selecting among their many templates.

The downside is that the themes are very rigid. For example, you don't always have a font choice. My teenage son described the look of this particular website as "retro" which is something you never want to hear from a Millennial.

The upside is that you can insert custom code, like a cookie script, which makes it preferable to Wix. It is currently priced at $14.95 per month. Smartphone version is easy enough to use but nothing special.

Figure 100. Website from Vistaprint.com

JimDo.com

JimDo is an easy to use do-it-yourself website creator that as of this moment costs $90 per year. It comes with a nicely formatted version for smartphones except that I had trouble getting a prominent click-to-call link into the smartphone version. This issue is enough for me to recommend against JimDo.

An example of a JimDo website that I built is shown in the next figure.

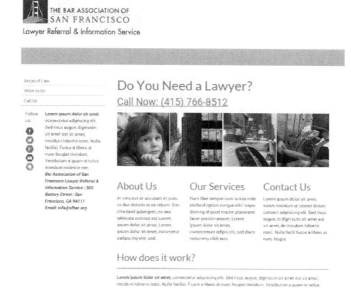

Figure 101. Website from JimDo.com.

Weebly.com

Weebly is another popular do-it-yourself website builder that I found easy to setup with a number of elegant themes. The smartphone version was less to my liking than Squarespace's mainly because, like the JimDo website, I couldn't figure out a way to add an easy to access click-to-call button.

Currently priced to move at $59 per year.

Figure 102. Example website from Weebly.com.

Themeforest

There are countless inexpensive templates at Themeforest (www.themeforest.net) to choose from, and but you'll need to be a little more experienced in website development to create something with visual appeal. The figure below shows a website that I created in a few days with stock photography that I bought in advance. You'll need to set up your own hosting.

Figure 103. Website using a template from Themeforest.net.

Off-shore website companies

For market research, I occasionally write back to website development companies in my spam folder to see what they offer. When I ask for a link to their portfolio, the quality of the work ranges from terrible to pretty good. The pricing varies a lot too and I find that with a little push back, the company will retreat from its price for Americans to something more in line with what their local competitors are charging.

Choose wisely because everything depends on the website.

If you're buying a custom website, make sure that it is "responsive"

As a final note, make sure that the company you choose builds the website to be "responsive." A responsive website is a website that "responds" to the width of the device that the visitor is using to access your website. For example, if someone comes to your website from their PC, the website knows to serve up

243

the full-size version of your website. If someone comes to your website on a handheld device like an iPhone, the website will render differently and much more narrowly so as to be easily viewed and navigated on a small screen.

Figure 104. Version of one of our responsive websites, shown here on an Android device.

If you're not sure which website is best for your specific business objectives, feel free to contact us at info@matejkamarketing.com, or you can call us at (415) 513-8736. We can discuss what your website needs are in the context of your existing website and your budgetary constraints.

> IMPORTANT: As soon as your website is live, install Google Analytics and Google Remarketing code so that you can start gathering critical data and start planting cookies on website visitors (whether you ever intend to use the cookies, it's good to have them in circulation just in case).

Evaluating the Performance of Your Website

Whether your website has been live on the web for years or was recently built, there's no substitute for stepping back and taking a look at how it's working for you.

Google Analytics

Do you have Analytics in your website? If not, have your website content manager insert the code into your website as soon as possible.[40]

If Analytics code has been in your website for a while, you will have data to look at. The more data you have to examine, the more complete picture you will get of how your website is doing.

Is your bounce rate under 50%? Are people spending at least a few minutes on your website? Are they viewing on average at least 2 pages per visit? Are people staying on some pages and bouncing from other pages?

What are your top exit pages? If it's your contact form, that may be a sign that there's a problem with your form.

What is the data for your "Thank You" page telling you? What is the percentage of people who navigate to the contact form and finally use it?

If your Analytics data is showing an 80% bounce rate and a visit duration of less than a minute, that's either a bad indicator for the attractiveness of your website or it may speak to the low quality of your traffic, or both.

Viewing this data over the longest possible period of time will give you a rough sense of what your visitors think of the pages of your site.

We go into Analytics with more specificity a little later in this chapter.

Your anecdotal referral source data

When you ask people how they found out about your firm, how often do they cite "web" or "Internet" or "Google" as their referral source? Each time someone makes any online reference, take that as a vote in favor of your website. Include a count of the email inquiries as votes in favor of the website.

If no one ever references your website or finding you online, it's either a sign that the website is driving people away or that no one can find it for its poor visibility. Sometimes it's both.

Often at my CLEs, lawyers will dismiss the Internet as a lead generator, saying something to the effect, "Most of my clients come from other attorneys, and my website has never gotten anything for me." This is a warning bell that their online lead generation system is underdeveloped. While your referral network may be the source of your best clients, Google should be the source of your most clients.

What to do if your data suggests that your lead generation system needs work.

If there are signs that your website isn't as productive as it should be, it doesn't necessarily mean that you need to throw everything away and get a new website. I have seen on several occasions an underperforming website improve to acceptable productivity levels by adding calls to action, tweaking the content, adding good stock photography, moving a contact form, getting a mobile version of the website in place, and the like.

A few items for your website to-do list if your website isn't productive enough

Is your website mobile ready?

What does your site look like on an iPhone? If you need to zoom in to read it or scroll left-to-right to see it all, then the website is not mobile-ready and needs to be.

How do you get one? It's easier and cheaper than most people would guess. Any competent web developer can create a mobile website for you without having to recreate your current website. Many hosting companies like Hostgator offer mobile website set up free of charge if you host it there for about $5 per month. If your website is hosted somewhere else, a list of hosting companies that provide similar services can be found at http://go.mobi/app/buy-a-gomobi-site/3563818/36/

If your website is built in WordPress, there are free plug-ins that will easily create a basic mobile version of your website. A very popular WordPress plug-in that will generate a highly functional mobile version of your website in minutes is called WPtouch.

Does your content reach out to your ideal client?

It may not be the look of your website that causes people to leave it before making contact with you. It may be how it's written.

Read your key pages, such as your homepage, bio, and practice area pages. Are they merely informational, or do they speak to people on a more personal level?

If your pages are purely about the law and don't convey any particular empathy for the people who are looking for legal help, it may not move people to reach out to you in the volume that it could.

If you decide to rewrite some of your pages, think about your ideal client type when you are creating content for your website and write to that person. The tone of your website is very important and will depend in part on your practice area. For example, a criminal defense attorney may want to exude a tone that the attorney is a passionate, tough-as-nails defender of civil rights, whereas a Medicaid lawyer may want to describe themselves as compassionate, caring and approachable.

We must also be mindful of what people want to know about us. It has been found that "Millennials" - an important group of 77 million Americans many of whom are already in their late 30s with children - are more interested in why you became a lawyer and what you do to help the community than where you went to law school.

Testimonials and case results

If allowed in your State, testimonials from satisfied clients can help visitors feel comfortable with you, and case results can give them confidence that you're the successful lawyer they've been looking for. If you don't have any on your website, there may be some good reviews of your law firm that you can copy from other review sites.

Figure 105. BASF LRIS testimonials page.

Calls to action

Visitors to your website often need to be told what to do next. A large, colorful button saying, "Contact us for a free consultation," can sometimes make a big difference. Contact forms throughout your website—in the same location on every page—can also motivate people to make contact with you in greater numbers.

Here are a few examples of calls to action.

Figure 106. "Learn How" and "Contact Us Today" calls to action.

In the figure above from an older version of my own website, notice the large "Learn How" button in the middle of the homepage that prompts the user to read more about our service offerings.

In the following figure, this lawyer's contact form is in the upper left-hand corner of every page, with the top banner displaying two calls to action: "Request a free consultation" above the contact form and "Call us" in the upper right corner.

Figure 107. Homepage, upper left contact form.

As another example, following is the homepage of the Houston Lawyer Referral Service, which I mention earlier in this book is among the highest producing legal websites in our current portfolio. This website has three prominent calls to action. The top navigation has a "Contact Us" link and two of the three images towards the bottom are labeled "Request a Lawyer Referral" and "Contact Us Today."

Figure 108. Three calls to action on the Houston Lawyer Referral Service's homepage.

Chat software

Chat software helps your website be more productive in a few ways. First, it gives people another avenue through which to reach out to you. Second, when you're "online," that is, signed in an available to chat, it lets the website visitor know that there are real people behind the website with whom they can communicate if they wish.

For chat, my recommendation is Zopim, although there are other comparable chat software solutions out there like Olark. Go to Zopim.com (or some other chat software vendor) and set up an account. They will give you a code that your website content manager will need to insert into every page on the website on which you want the chat bubble to appear.

You can add a thumbnail of yourself or your logo into the chat bubble, or if you prefer, you can leave it in its default state and it will look something like the next figure.

At about $15 per user per month, it's remarkably affordable. You or someone on your staff must be personally logged in to chat with people. Several law firms and bar associations I work with use the software, find it intuitive to use and like it.

Keeping it open in the background is easy enough, but you have to be ready to start a chat session when someone pings you.

Figure 109. Zopim chat dialogue balloon.

In the event that you'd prefer not to be on-call during business hours to chat with possible leads, there are other services that provide complete 24/7 chat coverage. Among these companies, my preference is ApexChat (apexchat.com).

ApexChat charges per chat session and their chat operators are well trained using a script that you can adapt to your needs. When the chat session is with a website visitor with an appropriate legal problem who gives their contact information to an ApexChat operator, it costs $25 per chat session last I heard. I have found them to be accommodating when I've pushed back about whether a chat session fits within the established criteria.

The look and placement of the chat box on your website is more flexible than one of its bigger competitors.

Other companies offer similar services and many offer identical services as resellers of ApexChat. If you're exploring 24/7 chat services you may want to go with a reseller who may be able to offer a per-chat rate lower than what ApexChat charges retail.

I encourage you to explore your various options, but Zopim is my recommendation for the lawyer on a shoestring.

Stock photography

If your website is underperforming, it may help to liven it up with some practice area-specific stock photography.

As we discuss elsewhere in this book, when selecting images for your site, avoid legal clichés like scales of justice, courthouse steps, and gavels. For your criminal defense page, a high-quality image of a police car can resonate for many defendants. A photo of a busy highway can work well for DUI/DWI and car accidents. For family law, nothing speaks to a family law client like photographs of happy children.

A vast inventory of royalty-free stock photography can be viewed and purchased at iStockPhoto or Shutterstock usually for about $30 per image. There are free stock photography websites and my favorite is PixaBay (https://pixabay.com/). The photos are mostly of high-quality and no attribution to the photographer is usually required.

Translate some or all of your website to Spanish or other languages spoken in your office.

If you speak Spanish or have someone in your office who speaks Spanish (or another language spoken by potential clients in your community), you have a terrific opportunity to reach the Spanish-speaking community, especially through Google advertising. If you have a lot of content translated, Google should also reward you for it in its organic results. In many markets, this population is underserved and can be reached relatively easily with very little competition.

There are click-to-translate applications, but it's preferred to manually translate the pages and put them in a Spanish language part of your website. This gives Google Spanish language content to index. Additionally, if you're advertising in Spanish, you can link your Spanish language ads directly to Spanish language pages. The inquiry rate when you bring someone searching in Spanish on a smartphone to a Spanish language page on your mobile website can be as high as 30%.

I have found that the Spanish-speaking community is especially likely to use mobile click-to-call. Consequently, it is very important to have a version of your website formatted for a mobile device, and that there be a click-to-call button visible on your website without having to scroll.

Add your accolades

Put your awards, memberships and other official-looking seals on your website to help establish your credibility and expertise.

A website beyond repair

If you feel like your website is beyond repair or if you're ready for a fresh look, fortunately, there is so much competition in the website development industry that websites are getting inexpensive and as we discussed earlier, there are lots of do-it-yourself options.

Remember that you can bring thousands of visitors to a flawed website and have nothing to show for it, and you can bring half as many visitors to a very good website and have a robust law practice. Make sure that you analyze your data closely and ask everyone how they found out about you when they call you. Without this information, you won't know whether your website works or not.

There is no timeline for the website build or facelift, as the case may be. It takes as long as it takes and is not to be rushed (unless the lead generation is urgent). Having your completed website as a good foundation will make the rest of the lead generation ecosystem worth the resources.

A little more about what your Analytics data is telling you about your traffic

One last thing before we continue with the traffic-generation part: while you have your Analytics dashboard open, let's take a look at how much traffic you're getting, where your visitors are coming from, and how they are responding to your website.

Google moves navigational elements around in Analytics periodically and changes the names of certain elements (e.g., recently "Visitors" was renamed "Sessions," and "Unique Visitors" became "Users").

Once logged in to your Analytics, from the default "Audience Overview" you can gather some cursory information about your website. We've already discussed this earlier in this book and touched on it earlier in this chapter and won't go into it in much detail here.

It's hard to generalize about whether your traffic level is where it should be because it depends on the population of your market and the demand for your practice areas. A personal injury lawyer in a large metropolitan area is going to have a large population of legal consumers and should get a lot of traffic to the website. Conversely, a rural law firm in a narrow practice area is going to get less traffic to their website regardless of how visible they make themselves.

One measure of whether you have adequate visibility is by looking at where your traffic is coming from.

Simply put, is Google your number one traffic source? Not that Google should be responsible for more than half of your traffic but that it should result in a greater amount of traffic than any other source. As was discussed earlier in this book, Google dominates law-related searches in the United States and should dominate your traffic sources as well. If you aren't getting a lot of your traffic from Google, then you're simply not visible enough in Google.

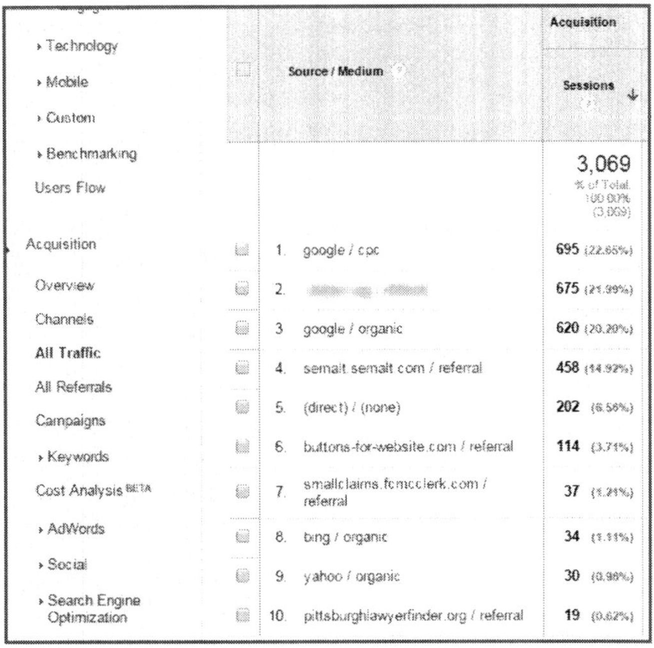

Figure 110. Top referral sources for a legal website in a medium-sized metropolitan community.

Notice in the figure above that Google is responsible for 45% of this legal website's traffic. In this chart, "google/cpc" refers to Google's pay-per-click advertising and "google/organic" refers to traffic the website is getting from visibility in Google's organic results.

One can conclude by looking at this figure that this website enjoys a lot of Google visibility, both in the index and in Google's sponsored listings, especially considering the medium-sized community that they serve.

It's never really enough, however. With thousands of daily law-related searches in Google in every community, there's always opportunity for more traffic, more leads, and more clients.

Google AdWords Advertising

Now that you have the website in place and have had a preliminary look at your traffic, it's time to start getting more traffic to your site.

Nothing delivers like Google advertising and with such immediacy, so we will begin there. The first step will be to build a Google advertising account and start running some ads.[41]

Go to www.google.com/adwords and click on the blue "Get Started Now" button.

Figure 111. Getting started with Google AdWords.

Go through the process step-by-step. Set up your first campaign (by default "Campaign #1") and then your first ad group. Initially, your first ad group can contain one ad.

259

Expanded Text Ads

An AdWords expanded text ad has specific character limits follows:

Expanded Text Ad Limits

	Expanded Text Ad Character Limit	Current Text Ad Limit
Headline 2	30 characters	NA
Description	Consolidated 80 character description	2 Description Lines with 35 character each
Display URL	Replaced with 2 path fields, each having 15 character limit and is an optional field	35 character limit

Figure 112. Google expanded text ad character limits.

Here is an example of an expanded text ad as it appears in a typical Google search result:

BBB Accredited Attorneys | Find the Top Rated Firms in SF | BBB.org
[Ad] www.bbb.org/GtrSF/Attorneys ▾
Search Your Better Business Bureau For A Lawyer You Can Trust Now!

Figure 113. Example of Google's expanded text ad.

Call-only Ads

Call-only ads are a different type of Google ad that appears only on smartphones and does not give the searcher an option to navigate through the ad to the law firm's website. I like these ads because, for the most part, clicks end up being phone calls to your office and in most locations, for most practice areas, I've found them to be more productive from a lead-generation standpoint than the expanded text ad.

Character limits

	Example ad	Limit for most languages
Business name:	Business name	25 characters
Phone number:	Call: (555) 555-5555	none
Description line 1:	Description line 1	35 characters
Description line 2:	Description line 2	35 characters
Display URL:	www.example.com	35 characters

Figure 114. Google call-only ad character limits.

Here is an example of a call-only ad as it would appear on a smartphone:

Call: (410) 919-9445
GilmanBedigian.com/Injury-Lawyers
Don't Fight Your Injury Case Alone!
Record-Setting Lawyers. Call 24/7.

Figure 115. Example of Google's call-only ad.

Keywords

Then you add "keywords" to each ad group, keeping as few keywords per ad group as possible so that your ads can be narrowly tailored to the user's search. For example, your ad group for divorce would have phrases like "divorce lawyer" and "divorce attorneys" and the like; and the ad group for custody would have phrases like "custody lawyers" and "custody attorney" and so on.

In the same way, the ads in the divorce ad group would focus on divorce and the ads in the custody ad group would focus on custody. And finally, the URL on the divorce ads would take people to your divorce page and the URL on the custody ads would take people to your custody page.

261

Continue building ad groups over time, keeping them as narrowly focused as possible and connect them to specific practice area pages created for this purpose.

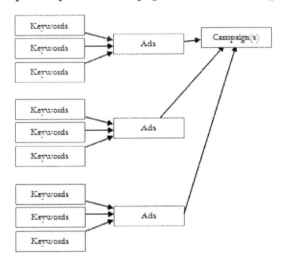

Figure 116. The basic structure of a Google advertising campaign.

Locations, bidding and budgets

Set your geographic target in "Settings" to your community if you have a local law practice. Set your daily budget and ad schedule. Choose a daily budget amount that makes sense to you, but do not make it too low. If your daily budget is lower than some of your bids, then Google may not run your ads that have max bids in excess of your daily budget.

The amount of your daily budget is largely practice area- and location-specific and it's hard to say here what may be reasonable in your particular circumstances. As a guideline, if you have a small overall budget, it is better to have a high daily budget and run your ads for only select hours of the week and/or select days of the month.

As of October 2017, Google will spend up to twice your daily budget to give the advertiser, nonsensically, "more flexibility." This requires that you monitor your daily spend with more frequency to ensure that you don't overspend for the month.

As for bidding, this is done initially at the ad group level, and Google requires that you set a bid at the time of ad group creation. Your bid will dictate to a certain extent what your cost per click is going to be. At first, your bid may be too low or too high and is largely a matter of trial and error. Your average position in Google's search results for that ad group will tell you whether your bid is at the right level.

ETHICS ALERT

Bidding on Law Firm Names in Google

When a law firm advertises in Google, the goal is to get as much local traffic to its website as possible that relates to its practice areas. To do this, the law firm casts the widest possible net by bidding on every conceivable, pertinent, law-related search phrase. In certain areas of law, like personal injury, the number of phrases bid-upon in a well-built campaign can be 2,000+

Over the years, among the more aggressive advertisers, it has been commonplace to bid on the names of other local law firms in the same practice area(s). For example, if you practice in the same area of law as the Johnson & Smith law firm, you can bid on the phrase "Johnson & Smith." Then, anytime someone searches for that law firm by name, they see the advertiser's ad and may click on it. If they click on your ad and you compare favorably against Johnson & Smith, it's a lead to the advertiser's law firm that may have otherwise gone to the other law firm.

While this has not been an uncommon practice among lawyers, lately there have been issues about this type of advertising.

State Bar Ethics Opinions

There has been at least one state bar that has issued an opinion about the practice of bidding on a competitor's name. The North Carolina State Bar in 2010 Formal Ethics Opinion 14 found that it was a violation of the Rules of Professional Conduct for a lawyer to bid on another lawyer's name in Internet search engine advertising.

Whether your state will ultimately follow North Carolina on this issue, it's hard to predict, but chances are that your state is a Model Rule state like North Carolina.

Case Law

Some law firms, when they become aware that other firms are bidding on their firm name, have been filing lawsuits claiming unfair competition, trademark infringement, and false advertising.

In a case reported in the ABA Journal in

October 2013, a Florida personal injury firm sued a competing law firm in federal court arguing unfair competition, trademark infringement, and violations of the Anti-Cybersquatting Consumer Protection Act.[2] If the case is finally resolved in favor of the plaintiffs, it will have an impact on whether any advertiser in the eleventh circuit dares to continue bidding on other law firms' names.[3]

Why not to do it

In the United States, Google has no restrictions on the practice of bidding on competitors' trademarks, and you're apparently free to do it in states that have not prohibited it yet. However, for the following reasons, I believe that the risks of this type of advertising outweigh the value of the potential return.

First, if very few people are searching for that law firm, it's possible that Google will seldom run the advertiser's ad on account of its low search volume. If Google only runs the ad once in a while, and if only 2% or 3% of Google users click on the ad, the advertiser probably will not get any significant traffic from it (except maybe from the competing law firm itself to get the address of the advertiser for its cease and desist letter).

Second, it's possible that Google will display one of the advertiser's ads on a search for one of its competitors based on Google's best guess at the user's search intent anyway. For example, if Google has a sense that the user is looking for a lawyer based on, among other things, previous searches in the user's search session, it possibly can deliver the advertiser's ad on a subsequent search for the competing law firm.

Third, the advertiser will invite an angry cease and desist letter, which could needlessly cost the advertiser a lot of time, headache, and attorneys' fees.

The practice of bidding on competitors' names may not yet be prohibited by local legislation or case law, but it is recommended that you as a Google advertiser not bother to bring upon yourself this potential trouble for such a low volume of traffic.

Google Remarketing

After you've created your first few ads and connected them to some important search phrase, now it is time to set up your "Remarketing" campaign.[42] This will be completely different from your search campaign. Rather than displaying your ads to people who are actively searching in Google for legal help, this campaign will display ads elsewhere on the Internet to people who have been to your website before or who match a profile of people who have been to your website before.

While logged into your AdWords account, go to "Shared library/Audiences."

Figure 117. Shared library to fetch Remarketing tag.

Follow the steps to get your Remarketing code, then Google will prompt you to email the insertion instructions to your website content manager. If that's you, put your email address into the box provided. Then follow the instructions in your email exactly as Google sets them out.

When the code is in your website, every visitor to your website will have a "cookie" implanted into their browser. Then Google can tell on other websites that this person had been on your website previously and show that person one of your ads.

ETHICS ALERT

When using Google Remarketing you are planting cookies on the browsers of visitors to your website. Your privacy policy should contain a section informing your visitors about that, something to the following effect.

"COOKIE USAGE

Please note that we may use cookies when you visit our website. We do not collect personally identifying information in this way. You can change your web browser's Internet preferences to disable or delete cookies although that may affect certain functions on this site. To learn how to manage your cookies, please follow the instructions from your specific browser."

Setting up the remarketing campaign

After the remarketing code has been inserted into every page on your website, you set up your Remarketing campaign. By putting one or more ads into this campaign, you'll tell Google what ads you want Google to display when they detect a person with one of your cookies on their browser.

You set up the campaign by going back to "All online campaigns" and clicking on the red "+Campaign" button. Choose "Display Network only" and follow the step-by-step instructions.

Figure 118. Setting up your Remarketing campaign.

Google will require that several hundred cookies be planted on the browsers of visitors before it will run any of your remarketing ads. It is expected that this will take a few months but can be sooner if your website receives a large number of visitors. The cookie script should be placed on every page of your website as soon as the Google account has been built to expedite the implantation of the cookies.

While you are waiting for the number of cookies to reach Google's threshold requirement, you'll have time to create text ads and banner images of up to 16 sizes to fit the size requirements of Google's affiliated ad display websites.

As we noted earlier, Google has been disabling remarketing campaigns for certain categories of law, like criminal defense. The enforcement of the policy is manual and apparently arbitrary, and most of my remarketing campaigns, even in sensitive practice areas, continue to run. So it's still worth it for you until Google shuts it down.

Bing/Yahoo Advertising

Bing and Yahoo advertising at this time are integrated about half of the time, so you advertise in both search engines through your Bing account. As we discuss elsewhere in this book, some of the time Yahoo ads come from Google and other times from Yahoo's own advertising platform, Gemini.

When you are creating your Bing advertising account for Bing/Yahoo advertising, you will notice that it is identical in nearly every respect to Google AdWords.

Marketing to the Spanish-Speaking Community

If you speak Spanish or have someone in your office that speaks Spanish, you have a terrific opportunity to reach the Spanish-speaking community through Google advertising.

In my experience with the Spanish language campaigns that my company runs for lawyers and bar associations, clicks in the Spanish language cost one-half to one-third of what comparable English language clicks cost. It will require that you translate portions of your website to Spanish and ideally, the entire website.

As I mention in a few other places in this book, I have found that the Spanish-speaking community is especially likely to use mobile click-to-call, almost to the exclusion of all other devices. Consequently, when advertising to the Spanish language community, it is important to have a version of your website formatted for smartphones.

Social Media

Now that your website is in place and you have some traffic and maybe a few leads coming through Google advertising, it's time to reach out to your community on a more personal level through your points of engagement - social media.

Social media for law firms consists usually of a Facebook Fan Page, Twitter account, Google+ business page, and LinkedIn Company Page. You may occasionally find a law firm with Pinterest or Instagram accounts as well.

A well-maintained presence on these platforms gives your law firm an online personality, establishes your law firm's expertise in your practice areas, and gives people online additional opportunities to make direct contact with you. Most importantly, social media gives you the opportunity to push your message out to your subscribers/followers.

Google indexes all of the four major social media platforms and apparently favors websites that have active and expanding social media content, thus further enhancing your credibility with Google and website visitors.

Figure 119. Familiar icons from the big four social media platforms.

The setup

The ease with which one can set up the four social media platforms varies, and there are a few prerequisites. For ease of setup, Twitter is relatively effortless whereas setting up your LinkedIn Company Page is more challenging.

To create a Facebook Fan Page, you need to have a personal Facebook page to attach it to, likewise with Google+ and LinkedIn.

The banner graphics for each platform should be similar in appearance to create a cohesive look among your various media. You'll find that the dimensions are completely different for each platform. This will create some work for your art department.

Get posting

Once you start posting regularly, it gets easier, albeit a little disruptive of your weekly routine. Twitter and Facebook are very easy to post to. While very few people are probably reading your Google+ feed, they are most likely to encounter that one if you post to it often. Google has made it clear in recent months that they will reward you for having an active Google+ account.

It is advised that you seldom make self-referential posts unless there is actually something newsworthy happening at your law firm. Some of your "Followers" may view too much self-promotion as off-putting and may unsubscribe. My company manages the social media accounts for about 20 law firms and bar associations and it is our practice to keep the self-referential posts to about one in 20 so as not to make their thousands of followers feel like the platforms are merely for marketing purposes.

Build connections

Active and deliberate gathering of "Likes" and "Followers" assure broad reach and authority in the social-sphere.

There are various techniques to get "Likes" and "Followers." A tip is that if you "Follow" and "Like" people, a lot of the time they will "Follow" and "Like" you back. In Twitter, if you follow the people who are following your competitors, you can connect with a more targeted audience because they have already expressed an interest in your subject matter.

Social media advertising can help get followers but this type of advertising is not otherwise recommended for reasons given earlier in this book.

Put the social media icons on your website and links in your email signature lines.

Social media icons will help increase visitors' comfort levels and make it possible for them to read more about you. "Share" buttons allow website visitors to easily share your content with others in their social networks. "Follow" buttons will make it easy for people to subscribe to your social media feeds.

To keep your Ecosystem development as deliberate and on-schedule as possible, try to have the build-out of the social media accounts, including the creation of all of your banner and logo graphics, complete soon after your website is good to go.

Thereafter, you should plan to post a few times per week per platform. You can post on law-related information, legal news items of interest, happenings of note at your firm and community events.

Content Creation

Evaluate the content that you currently have on your website. Is it informative and high-quality? Do you have enough of it?

We talked earlier in this book about the importance of Landing Pages for your Google advertising. In this section we address whether you have enough practice area content and what you should blog about. Set up a blog on your website if you do not have one and commit yourself to creating a few blog posts per month. I find it easy to blog in my car during my morning commute to my office. By speaking into the voice recorder of my smartphone, a member of my staff transcribes, edits and posts the new content to my website.

You can write many in advance and schedule them to automatically publish if your website is on WordPress. By having lots of high-quality, informative content on your website, you establish yourself as an important information resource to Google. Thus, you will be more likely to show up in Google's search results when a user is searching for information related to one of your blog posts.

As for practice area pages, think about subdividing them as narrowly as possible. For example, if you are a criminal defense lawyer, you may create pages for theft crimes, drunk driving offenses, assault crimes, misdemeanors, disorderly conduct, and so on. Likewise, if you are a personal injury lawyer, you may want to subdivide your vehicle accidents page to truck accidents, bicycles, motorcycles, and the like.

In addition to your written content, commit yourself to creating videos once in a while, streaming those videos to the content on your website that is related to the subject matter of your videos.

Paid Directory Listings

In an earlier chapter we addressed how to calculate the value of a directory listing. Using that formula, I have found most directories to be overpriced.

There are inexpensive exceptions where the traffic outweighs the cost of the listing for most practice areas. For example, a number of county bar associations operate local legal directories under the name of "FindaLawyer." An example of one is ColumbusFindaLawyer.org, operated by the Columbus Bar Association. I have found these local, bar-operated directories of value and I recommend a listing if your county bar operates one.[43]

As another example, I found a DUI directory that charges only a fraction of what the listing seemed to be worth, and I have recommended the directory to my DUI clients.

A variety of online Yellow Pages want to sell ad placement on their websites. I always recommend against these types of paid listings because they offer free listings too. Their sales people often forget to mention that.

Better Business Bureau (BBB)

Among the paid directories, the BBB directory is one that I recommend. BBB is the only local directory that is experiencing any significant year-over-year growth. It's known to be an important trust factor for Google (which is good for search rankings) and it appears to be a growing resource for consumers for some reason.

The paid BBB listing comes with the familiar BBB seal.

Figure 120. Variations of the BBB seal.

It's hard to concretely measure the value of the BBB seal because there are 3 things we're buying here: (1) probably a little bit of direct traffic, (2) the seal, which bolsters your law firm's trustworthiness among consumers, and (3) the benefit you get from Google through your website's association with the BBB website.

The price of the BBB seal varies by community and is based on the number of employees your law firm has. I've seen it at around $300 per year for a one-person business in smaller population areas.

You'll want to evaluate the direct traffic to your website and keep an eye on whether the BBB traffic growth continues.

Free Directory Listings

Add your law firm to each of the important free directories, starting with the five directory aggregators (Localeze, Infogroup, Axciom, Foursquare and Factual), using a consistent name-address-phone convention until your firm is included in all of the important directories.

If your law firm is found to already be listed in one of the directories, make sure that the listing conforms to your law firm's name-address-phone convention. If you find that there are duplicate entries, claim and remove the extra ones so that you have only one listing in each directory.

YouTube Video Creation and Advertising

Millions of Millennials, who are heavy video-content consumers, are approaching 40 years old and aging fast. Reaching this demographic group is important and will become increasingly so as millions more continue to come of age.

Make a video

Make time (maybe once per month) to create short videos about your firm and practice area(s). If you're not sure what to say on a video, just rehearse reading a page of your website until you can recite it without looking away from the camera.

You can advertise for a videographer on websites like Craigslist and Upwork (until recently it was known as eLance). You can probably find skilled and talented people there who will come to your office with their equipment for not very much money.

If you are truly on a tight budget, find someone in your office with an iPhone, put it on a windowsill on a sunny day, and start recording.

If you're camera shy, you can do a voice-over for a slideshow—just be mindful of the sound quality. Absent that, you can have a voiceless slideshow for people to read about your law firm in a video format and add some free background music.

In any case, you will need someone who can edit video, and this is something you'll probably have to pay for unless you're lucky enough to have someone like this on staff.

YouTube Director

In Fall of 2016, Google introduced a service called "YouTube Director" (https://director.youtube.com/) It's intended to help small businesses create a 30 to 45 second video for purposes of advertising on YouTube.

The way it works is that you create a short script using Google's template and they send a filmmaker to your office to shoot and edit a video for you on-site. The YouTube Director videos that I've coordinated for my clients are of remarkable quality.

The service is free of charge except that you must commit to spending at least $150 in YouTube advertising at some point in the future. Then you own it and can use it for whatever purpose suits you (especially to stream it on your homepage to personalize your firm).

As of January 2017, it's only offered in seven cities – San Francisco, Los Angeles, Chicago, Atlanta, Boston, New York (New York County only) and Washington D.C. My Google representative tells me that they have plans to expand to other cities eventually and you should check to see if they are in your area yet.

In the event that you are not in one of their service areas, they also have a do-it-yourself YouTube video app for iPhone and iPad (ironically not for Android as of now). I haven't had a chance to see how it works but if you want to give it a try, it's free and can be found in the Apple's App Store if you search for "YouTube Director for Business."

Set up your law firm YouTube channel

Setting up a YouTube channel is much easier than it used to be now that Google has connected your YouTube account to your Google+ account. I am not going to go into the details of the process here but hopefully you'll figure it out.

Call me at (415) 513-8736 or write to me at info@matejkamarketing.com if you need a little guidance with this.

Stream a video to your law firm website

YouTube makes it easy to embed a video into a page on your website. The following figure shows where to go to get the code that you will need for your website to stream the video. While viewing the video, click on the icon with the word "Share" next to it, and next choose "Embed" from among your three options. Then all you need to do is place the code into the source code of the website page where you want the video to show.

Figure 121. Getting the code to embed a YouTube video.

Be sure to click on the "Show More" button and unselect the checkbox labeled "Show suggested videos when the video finishes." This will prevent YouTube from showing other YouTube videos on your website after your visitors view the videos that you have embedded. See the next figure to view the location of this checkbox.

Share **Embed** Email

<iframe width="560" height="315" src="https://www.youtube.com/emb

Preview:

Video size: 560 × 315 ▾

☐ Show suggested videos when the video finishes
☑ Show player controls
☑ Show video title and player actions
☐ Enable privacy-enhanced mode [?]

Figure 122. Restricting YouTube to streaming your own videos only.

Post about the video periodically

Post about your video periodically in your social media but not too often because of the "self-referential" warning explained earlier.

Link to the video in your email signature

Linking to your video in your email signature line gives recipients an opportunity to click through to your video.

Advertise the video in YouTube

YouTube allows you to advertise your video for law-related searches, giving your law firm's video top-placement and providing cheap exposure. YouTube advertising is inexpensive (currently around $0.07 per view) and with the right video, you can get your message in front of thousands of YouTube users in your community for very little money.

YouTube video creation should be an ongoing effort, and if you put yourself on a set schedule on various practice area topics of interest to local consumers over the course of the year, you will be doing a lot to enhance your Ecosystem.

It's important to link your YouTube channel to your AdWords account so that you can add a call to action and link to your website to your video.

Online Review Management

Perform an initial online review audit set up alerts in Yelp and Google so that you know when a new review is posted.

The elicitation of positive Yelp, Facebook and Google+ reviews should be ongoing effort, with the goal of obtaining maybe one additional positive review per month. Aim for about 7 to 10 5-star reviews in each review site, keeping your overall star rating as close to 5-stars as possible.

Get Positive Reviews

There are techniques for getting positive reviews that we discuss earlier in this book.

Damage Control

If someone has posted a negative review about your law firm, reach out to them privately to see if there's a way to make things better. If they aren't responsive to that sort of thing, you can post a public response of apology and explanation. If the negative review falls within one of several certain categories at Yelp, you can request an editorial review to have it removed by Yelp.

Create an e-Newsletter

Email marketing (e-Newsletters) is the most direct point of engagement. It works if done well and is free except for staff time. Law firms need a "sign up for our newsletter" box to collect email addresses of those interesting in receiving the newsletters.

To be in compliance with anti-spam laws, my understanding is that recipients of your newsletters need to affirmatively opt in before you send them anything.

For creating the newsletter, bulk email services like MailChimp (mailchimp.com) and Constant Contact have e-newsletter templates in which you just put in your graphics and content. My preference is for MailChimp because it's easy to use, has many good templates to choose from, and is free up to 2,000 email addresses.

Make sure to cross-promote your YouTube Channel and social media in the newsletter too.

You don't need to put anything in the newsletter about your services and how you can help them with their legal problem. Your newsletter is purely informational. It is to engage and inform the recipients while keeping your law firm's name and logo in their minds and in their email inboxes.

Many companies that send out e-newsletters report that e-newsletters can be effective in branding and client acquisition. You can also use it for your cause marketing. By sending out useful community service information, you can create goodwill towards your firm from your newsletter subscribers, as well as the local public services you're helping promote.

Your email list does not have to be very large to get started. Once you have 20 or 30 email addresses gathered, then go to mailchimp.com and get started. MailChimp is free for up to 2,000 email addresses and renders your newsletters well on mobile devices. It's easy enough to use and has a number of templates that are plug-and-play. The following figure shows a newsletter I created announcing a Matejka Marketing webinar using a simple MailChimp template.

ETHICS ALERT

Enacted in 2003, CAN-SPAM sets rules for commercial email and provides recipients with the right to request to stop getting emails. To ensure your email marketing is compliant, senders begin by always honoring opt-out requests, not using false or misleading information, and monitoring all mail sent on your law firm's behalf for authenticity.[44]

Figure 123. Newsletter created in MailChimp.

If you're using MailChimp, you'll need to create a banner 600 px wide and other images that are 160 px wide (height doesn't matter).

What to include in your newsletter:

A community events section would be unique to your area. Legal news and frequently asked questions could be adapted from online news sources or taken from your blog.

If you subscribe to local community newsletters and legal newsletters, you'll have more than enough content to adapt for your newsletter.

You'll only want to send newsletters maybe three or four times per year. If you send more than that, people may unsubscribe or send it to spam. I know I do.

Finally, make sure that your newsletter looks good on mobile devices. Your newsletter will if you're using one of MailChimp's templates.

Chapter 16. Closing the Deal

It's presumed that we all know how to close a deal. You've probably been practicing law for a while and your practice has been doing well so far.

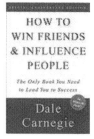

But just in case, if you haven't done so yet, please read this book. It's a quick read and will help.

The reason for this chapter is because the online consumer since the smartphone revolution has been found to be an impatient demographic. This new consumer-type demands immediate satisfaction in the micro-moment of their buying process.

The second part of this chapter is just some basic Telephone Sales 101 in case you would like a refresher on getting people into your office once you have them on the telephone.

The Golden 5 Minutes

It was found in a study by the two major universities that you have about 5 minutes to get back to someone following their initial contact with your law firm.

Please answer the phone

If a legal consumer calls you directly, someone needs to be there to answer the phone. A "hot connect" is always the best because the issue of getting back to them in a timely manner is taken out of the equation.

Another good reason why you want to pick up that phone is because they cannot talk to any of your competitors while you have them on the line. Learn from the plumber: it doesn't matter how deep in the muck they are, the plumber will always stop what they're doing to answer their phone. They know that voicemail is often a lost lead.

Get back to them immediately

Once people have come to your website and made contact with you, then it's all on you. They've already read about you on your website and have shown an interest in talking with you about their legal matters. If it takes a long time for you to respond to their inquiry, you may lose them to a competitor. Furthermore, once you do make contact with them, if your tone isn't friendly, thoughtful and professional, they may keep looking.

People expect an "immediate" response after their initial inquiry. What "immediate" means in this context is this: if a person finds you on the web and calls your law firm during business hours, someone at your office, whether it is you, a paralegal, or your receptionist, should answer the phone.

If you receive an email or a submission through your contact form from a viable prospect, it's a race between you and the other attorneys that person has contacted, so you need to respond very quickly.

They will be frustrated if it takes too long to hear from you, and it will be too late if they have had a meaningful conversation with someone else already.

In the following figure, you'll see that your window of opportunity is 5 minutes. It is four times less likely that you will make contact with someone if you wait 10 minutes to do so. If you wait until the next morning, it is sixty times less likely that you will ever make contact with them.

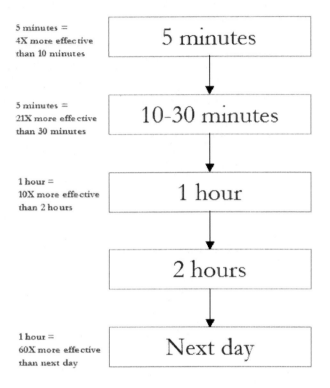

Figure 124. The Golden 5 Minutes.

Tips to Help Get That Online Consumer into Your Office

We established that you have a very short period of time to get back to people when they make contact with you. Now let's say that you have them on the phone because they either called you directly or you successfully got back to them before some other attorney had a good conversation with them. Here are some tips to help you get that person to stop looking for another lawyer.

At the point of initial contact you should introduce yourself and be brief and friendly. Tell them in a sentence or two about yourself and tell them what you know about them if anything at all. For example, if they made contact with you by email you might say, "I see from your email that you are looking for a lawyer who may be able to give you some advice about your injury."

Then you want to get them to start talking. Ask them an open-ended question or two to get them to talk about themselves or what they need. During this part, don't say anything; just take notes and occasionally let them know that you're still listening.

If it seems at the outset that this is someone who may be a good client for you, let them keep talking for a while before you start asking questions that will help you assess their case.

Once they have an opportunity to speak freely to someone who is listening, they will already start to get the sense that you care about their legal matter.

At this point you can start asking more specific questions to find out whether this is someone you can actually help. Don't talk about yourself yet. The conversation should still focus on the potential client and the circumstances of their legal matter.

Once you have a sense of the important details of their case, you'll probably have a good idea whether this is someone you can help. If it's not, here is an opportunity to refer this person to a colleague. If you have a sense that this is not a case that any of your colleagues would be interested in or if you don't know any lawyer who practices in this area of law, refer them to your local bar association's lawyer referral service.

If it looks like you'll be able to help them, now would be the time to explain why you are the attorney they should hire. You have already conveyed that you care over the course of the first few minutes when you actively listened to them. You further established your interest in their case in the second part of the conversation by asking pertinent questions.

Now in the third part of the phone call, summarize what you have heard and give them a brief synopsis of what you might recommend as a course of action. Tell them about similar successful cases that you have handled.

Do not expect to close the client during the phone call. The objective here is to get them into your office so that you can explain your unique value proposition and convey empathy towards their legal situation that may be hard to get across over the phone.

Once you have them in your office, your normal sales process kicks in. What has worked in the past should continue to work in the future. This may be the time to be candid about how long it will take, the steps you will need to go through to get a successful outcome, the kind of help that you will need from them, and of course, how much it might cost.

If you can get them to sign the retainer agreement, fantastic. Otherwise, follow up with them by email a few hours after your first meeting to thank them and to let them know again that you care and want to help. And continue on the sales cycle as always.

If you haven't done so yet, please read *How to Win Friends and Influence People*, by Dale Carnegie. It's required reading for every lawyer. It will make a difference.

Chapter 17. Ethics and Your Online Content

Ethics and Your Website Content

No attorney communications marketing your availability for legal services should be made on the web without a thorough understanding of your local rules of professional conduct relating to attorney advertising. This chapter covers the importance of disclaimers and privacy policies on law firm websites and is a survey of the variations among the various states on these issues.

This is not intended to be a comprehensive survey, nor should it be relied upon as current or complete as to your particular State. Please review your local rules as they pertain to your practice areas.

All references in this chapter to the rules of professional conduct are to the Model Rules of Professional Conduct (Model Rules) drafted by the American Bar Association, adopted by almost every State substantially unchanged.

While we're discussing primarily the Model Rules, we're going to cover occasionally how they are applied differently from State to State.

The Rules and the Formal Opinions that we cover apply generally to all of your content, in print, billboards and what not, but for our purposes here, we focus on the digital content you create towards the development of your online leads ecosystem.

As you've seen throughout this book, developing your online leads ecosystem is in large part the creation of content about your law practice and making it available to legal consumers and search engines using various channels. Whether the content is distributed through your blog, social media, YouTube channel or by any other medium, we must stay cognizant that your local rules of professional conduct will apply to all content that is a "communication about the lawyer or the lawyer's services" (Rule 7.1).

Rule 7.1 - False or Misleading

Model Rule 7.1 is as follows, although it may vary somewhat in your State.

> *A lawyer shall not make a false or misleading communication about the lawyer or the lawyer's services. A communication is false or misleading if it contains a material misrepresentation of fact or law, or omits a fact necessary to make the statement considered as a whole not materially misleading.*

Rule 7.1 prohibits "false or misleading" communications. What is "false" is obvious and we won't spend any time on it. We wouldn't say anything in our communications that is untruthful and we, as lawyers, don't need a rule to tell us not to lie in our content. We hold ourselves to a higher standard than that.

But what is meant by "misleading?"

"Misleading" is dependent to some extent upon the sophistication of your visitors and the Model Rules attempt to protect even the least sophisticated among them. Since we can expect that legal consumers of all varieties will eventually happen upon your website, we need to cater to all people when making sure that no one is mislead by your content.

In the Model Rules, and in the 49 States (not California) that have adopted the Model Rules, Rule 7.1 prohibits false or misleading communications about our legal services. This prohibition includes truthful statements we make the nature of which may be misunderstood by a layperson.

We are going to get more specific in the next section about some categories of statements that have been determined to be misleading under the Model Rules and in some of the States' interpretation thereof.

Misleading Communications

In the context of what may be "misleading" about your ecosystem content, there are five topics we cover in this chapter:

- Is the content in your ecosystem legal information or legal advice?

- Are case results and testimonials guarantees of a similar outcome?

- Are we establishing an attorney-client relationship through the contact that we're making through the website?

- Does 'contingency fee' mean free of charge?

- What does it mean if you describe yourself as a "Specialist?"

Legal Information vs. Legal Advice

Suppose someone comes to your website. They're reading your blog or reading through a practice area page, and they think they know all they need to know to proceed with their case without consulting with a lawyer. They might conclude, "Okay, I don't need a lawyer now I know what to do."

We certainly don't want anyone relying to their detriment on what they read on our website or what they see anywhere else in our Ecosystem. Not only might it expose us to lawsuits for malpractice (however unmeritorious), we don't want our E&O insurance company getting wind of this sort of thing.

How do we manage the expectations of people who read our content? How do we get them to understand that when they enter our ecosystem, what they're reading is legal information, not legal advice?

We do that through easy-to-understand disclaimers. ABA Formal Opinion 10-457 discusses the various ways that people may be misled by content on your website and specifically recommends phrasing your disclaimer in lay terms that less sophisticated website visitors will easily understand.

To make sure people understand that your website content is legal information, not advice, prominent in your disclaimer should clearly express something to the following effect:

> *What you're reading on this website is legal information, not legal advice. Everyone's facts and circumstances are different. The information you are reading here is no substitute for talking to a lawyer and getting legal advice specific to your situation.*

Guest Blogging and Social Media

Some websites give you an opportunity to answer consumers' legal questions. Avvo and Quora are examples. A potential client might post a question, maybe a legal issue that they are grappling with, and they need a little background on what the law is. If you're answering specific questions in one of those forums, please make sure that you are leaving answers to questions couched in hypotheticals. In addition, always note in your answers that you are providing legal information, not legal advice, and that your response is not a substitute for talking to a lawyer about their particular facts and circumstances.

Perhaps they ask, "What's the statute of limitations for my car accident case?" Your answer might be: 'Oftentimes when someone gets injured in an auto accident, these [certain statutes] may apply. Your facts may be such that your statute of limitations is completely different. Please talk to a lawyer to find out for sure how long you have to sue."

All content that we add to our ecosystem, including our social media and YouTube videos can also be misperceived as legal advice. As such, we need to be liberal in our use of disclaimers so that no one is mislead and relies to their detriment on something you wrote or said.

It is easy enough to include a disclaimer in a YouTube video but it is harder to disclaim content in social media. For example, a Twitter post cannot exceed 140 characters, making the inclusion of an appropriate disclaimer practically impossible.

Be careful about what you post. It is safest to consider whether a social media post may be misperceived as legal advice before you post it. If you think there is a possibility that someone may take it as legal advice, post it with a disclaimer if space permits, and don't post it at all if space restrictions won't allow an appropriate disclaimer.

Case Results

Often you'll see on personal injury and criminal defense websites a page that's dedicated to all of the great results that the law firm has achieved for its past clients.

On a personal injury website you may see something like this: *"Brain Injury – 6 Million Dollar Verdict"* and *"Millions Recovered For Our Clients."* The Model Rules don't have a problem with case results as such, but they note that case results can be misleading if they cause a person to form an unjustified expectation that the same results could be obtained for them.

For example, let's say that someone searching for a lawyer for a brain injury case comes to a personal injury website. They go to the case results page and see that the firm got $6 million for a past brain injury plaintiff. Might that cause a visitor to that website to form an expectation that they would get 6 million dollars for their brain injury if they hired that firm?

What do we do about that, short of removing the case results from our websites altogether? We need to manage their expectations through our disclaimer.

Many States allow case results with appropriate disclaimers. Other States prohibit the use of case results altogether and we get into that later in this chapter.

As with the disclaimer about legal information vs. legal advice, we want to make sure that the case results disclaimer, as much as possible, is worded so as to be easily understood by unsophisticated visitors. If your disclaimer reads like a boilerplate EULA with statements about "warranties of fitness," that's not a good thing.

For case results, it may be simply a matter of stating *"Prior case results do not guarantee a similar outcome."* Your State may have specific language that you need to use and you should research it to be sure. It is recommended, and sometimes required, that the case results disclaimer be placed at the bottom of your case results page. I also recommend that you include it in your main disclaimer which would link from the footer of your website pages.

Testimonials

Many websites have testimonials from past satisfied clients to show that the firm is liked by people it has helped in the past. Elsewhere in this book, I talk about how testimonials can help in the effort to get your website to convert 15% of its visitors into inquiries..

From an ethics perspective, with respect to what is misleading, a lot of what applies to case results in the previous section is true for testimonials too.

The Model Rules don't speak specifically to testimonials. Many States allow testimonials and some States do not. If your State allows testimonials, like California, the State may have an explicit disclaimer requirement. In the case of California, there is prescribed language for the testimonial disclaimer as follows:

> *This testimonial or endorsement does not constitute a guarantee, warranty or prediction regarding the outcome of your legal matter.*

The wording of this disclaimer is simple, concise and probably understood by all. It is recommended that you use the disclaimer as California has drafted it unless your State has its own prescribed wording. California also requires that this disclaimer be placed on the testimonials page.

While you should do your research on this point and my information may not be current, some examples of States that I have found where you cannot use testimonials include Florida, Indiana and South Carolina. There are probably others.

Some states like Pennsylvania allow certain types of testimonials and prohibit others.

The bottom line here is if you plan to have case results and/or testimonials on your website, first research your local rules to see if they are allowed. If they are allowed, make sure you have your disclaimers in place, whether your State requires the disclaimers or not.

Establishing an Attorney-Client Relationship

Continuing on the topic of what is "misleading," we need to consider whether someone who makes contact with you through your website thinks they are establishing an attorney-client relationship.

There are several reasons why we want to do everything we can to manage the expectations of website visitors on this point. First, if they have an expectation that we are working towards the establishment of an attorney-client relationship (not necessarily establishing it but thinking that the process has begun), the information that they send you must be kept confidential.

Second, any information that you give them in return may have cause them to think that the information you sent is legal advice. As an example, if someone asks you a question by email and you send an answer back to them that is not hypothetical in nature, and is specific to their circumstances, then they might rely on what you said and act upon it in the furtherance of their case, possibly detrimentally, whether they hire you or not.

Third, if the client thinks you are their attorney and sends you sensitive information, you're precluded from representing an adverse party.

It has been reported that there are litigants who make contact with many lawyers for the very specific purpose of preventing those lawyers from representing an adverse party in their case. Here's how it works:

Let's say you have a great reputation in your community for divorce law and the soon-to-be-ex-husband doesn't want you or anyone like you in the community representing his soon-to-be-ex-wife. The husband in this scenario may spend a few hours sending contact form submissions to every divorce lawyer in the area, ostensibly to establish an attorney-client relationship, but with no actual plan to hire anyone (except for the lawyer whom he has already retained).

He sends enough sensitive information to give the attorneys who receive the contact form submission the idea that it's a viable lead. The attorney reaches back to begin the process of establishing an attorney-client relationship. Maybe a little more sensitive, but not damaging, information is sent to the lawyer. Through this process, the attorney who received the sensitive information has been "tainted."

The New York City Bar has a formal opinion on this practice (Association of the Bar of the City of New York Committee on Professional and Judicial Ethics Formal Opinion 2001-1 (2001)), referring to these litigants as "taint shoppers."

Going back to ABA's Formal Opinion 10-457, with respect to people forming an unjustified expectation that an attorney-client relationship is being established online, there are two trouble-spots of which lawyers need to be aware.

The first is through a website visitor's actual use of your contact form. Normally lawyers will have a contact form on their websites (which I highly recommend because we want people to be able to make contact with you as easily as possible by their preferred method, whatever that may be). We should be careful about what kind of information your contact form requests of the client. Is there anything in your contact form that requests information that a website visitor may consider sensitive?

There has been at least one instance where a law firm's contact form was found to be detailed enough that a visitor may form an expectation that the information being requested would remain confidential (Iowa State Bar Association Ethics Opinion 07-02). If the law firm's contact form gets into too much detail, then it may indeed create a feeling among some website visitors that they are filling out an intake.

Sometimes I'll see a checkbox on an attorney's contact form that says something to the following effect:

> *By checking this box, I understand that, through use of this contact form, no attorney-client relationship is being created.*

This is not a bad practice.

The second trouble-spot is when someone sends an unsolicited email and you respond. There is little you can do to manage the expectations of people who simply use your email address, so why might it be a problem? If the email link is on your website, then they may form the same expectation as with your contact form that their information will be kept confidential (Massachusetts Bar Association Opinion 07-01 (2007); Arizona State Bar Opinion 02-04 (2002)).

But what if you don't have your email address on your website and you get an unsolicited email from someone who received your email from a friend or an online directory?

If you write back and request more information from the client, then the client may form an expectation that a bilateral communication towards the establishment of the relationship has commenced. ABA Formal Opinion 10-457 notes

> *A telephone, mail or e-mail exchange between an individual seeking legal services and a lawyer is analogous. In these contexts, the lawyer takes part in a bilateral discussion about the possibility of forming a client-lawyer relationship and has the opportunity to limit or encourage the flow of information. For example, the lawyer may ask for additional details or may caution against providing any personal or sensitive information until conflicts check can be completed.*

In light of the above, when we are replying to an email from a prospective client, we want to make sure that they understand, prominently in the text of your outbound email, that this is legal information, not legal advice, and that we don't have an attorney-client relationship until you come into our office and we have a signed agreement.

In your full disclaimer page, you should have a section in there that basically says, *"Contacting us does not constitute an attorney-client relationship. Please do not send us any confidential information until we have a signed retainer agreement."*

Statements About Contingency Fees

Often personal injury attorneys will have statements on their websites to the effect of *"No fees until we win."* With respect to statements like this, we're going to go back to Rule 7.1, which states that a communication is misleading if it omits a fact necessary to make the statement not misleading. While the Model Rules do not speak specifically to the misleading nature of contingency fee statements, many States do. This is an issue that you definitely want to research locally.

What is misleading about contingency *"No fees unless we win,"* or *"We don't charge you fees unless we win your case,"* or something like that? It's misleading because a lot of the time, the client is responsible for litigation costs. On its face, the simple contingency fee statement, unqualified, may lead a lot of visitors to a personal injury website (or other type of plaintiff's law firm website) to think that hiring the lawyer won't cost them anything, whether they win or lose. In fact, depending on how the law firm structures its retainer agreement, the client may be on the hook for expert witnesses, filing fees, printing and what not. So, at the end of the case, assuming a successful outcome, the lawyer shaves the costs off the top, and splits the rest 60/40.

The statement *"No fees unless we win,"* is materially misleading without the qualifying statement about costs, when applicable. Some States specifically say that it's a violation of Rule 7.1 not to include the qualifying statement. The States that I'm aware of that have spoken to it require an additional disclosure. California phrases the disclosure in its comment to Proposed Rule 7.1 as follows:

> *A communication that states or implies "no fee without recovery" is misleading unless such communication also expressly discloses whether or not the client will be liable for costs.*

What is curious about this restriction is that I've never seen the contingency fee statement correctly phrased on any lawyer's website. I've seen the contingency fee statement on many personal injury websites, but I never see the second part - *"but, by the way, you'll be responsible for costs, whether we win or not."*

While California may seem like an extreme example, this is actually a typical formulation of the disclaimer. Research your local rules, and if you do have a contingency fee statement on your website, if your State speaks to it, you're going to want to qualify that statement with a disclaimer that the client (if they are) is responsible for costs. Later in this chapter, I've listed the States that I'm aware of that require the qualification for contingency fee statements, but my list may be incomplete.

Since marketing lawyers and bar associations is all I do, when I have a personal injury firm in a State that has this restriction, I prefer to remove the contingency fee statement altogether rather than adding the required addendum to be in compliance with the local rules. To be in full compliance would set you apart, in a negative way, from all of the contingency fee lawyers in your community who disregard or are unaware of the rule.

Are You a "Specialist"?

Rule 7.4 of the Model Rules speaks to the use of the word "Specialist" and "Specialization" in certain areas of law. Different States have different ways of interpreting this, but for the most part, as nearly as I can find, most States have taken Rule 7.4 exactly as it's formulated by the ABA.

> *Lawyers shall not state or imply that they are a Certified Specialist in a particular field of law unless the Lawyer has been certified as a Specialist by an organized that has been approved by an appropriate State authority, or that has been accredited by the American Bar Association. -- (Excerpt from Rule 7.4, Model Rules).*

When we are describing ourselves as a "Specialist," we need to make sure that the State recognizes the certifying body. If there is no certifying body, then we don't use the word. As with everything else we cover here, please check your local rules to see how they have modified Rule 7.4.

There are instances where a law firm unwittingly describe themselves as "specialists." "I'm a criminal defense specialist," or "I specialize in family law." Unless you're actually an appropriately certified specialist under Rule 7.4, then you want to get that word off your website and out of your marketing materials.

There are different ways of expressing the same idea. For instance, you can say "We focus on divorce law," or "Our law practice is exclusive to criminal defense."

Besides "specialist," there are other adjectives that you may use to describe yourself that may be seen as "misleading" under your local rules. In Ohio, for example, Rule 7.1 prohibits communications that are "false, misleading or non-verifiable," like "best," "cheapest," or "most effective."

The use of the word "expert," is restricted in many States, e.g., Iowa, Mississippi, Ohio and Virginia. Other States like California, haven't spoken to its use yet (as nearly as I can tell).

To be safe, when marketing lawyers, I specifically avoid the word "expert" in favor of some other adjective that will get the same idea across.

Tennessee is particularly restrictive on qualifiers that they see as misleading. In a 2004 formal opinion from their Ethics Committee, they conclude,

> *Lawyers may not claim that they are 'Number One,'*
> *'One of The Best,' 'Better,' the 'Top,' 'Excellent,'*
> *'Qualified,' 'Highly Qualified,' 'Experienced,'*
> *'Reputable,' 'Efficient,' or 'Preferred,' as such claims*
> *are unverifiable."*

As another example, Virginia says point-blank in a 2001 formal opinion:

> *"Lawyers may not claim to be an expert or to have expertise."*

I make a special note here about Florida. That State has made some curious changes and additions to the Model Rules. If you practice in Florida, please do your research before you rely on anything you read here. I will never hold myself out as an "expert" in Florida ethics.

It's worth emphasizing again that local rules apply not just to the content of your website. The restrictions apply equally to the content of your social media, how you describe yourself at Avvo and Yelp, your advertising, printed material and anywhere else your content may be (to the extent that you have control over it).

Reality Check

In the real world, is the disclaimer enough to manage the expectations of your website visitors? Are we indeed clarifying everything on our website so that, however unsophisticated the website visitor is, they aren't mislead by anything they read on your website?

I would suggest that while it would be ideal for people to read your disclaimer and understand it, and to have their expectations managed thereby, a lot of people just won't read it. Your website analytics will show that it is an infrequently visited page. For many, it's like an end-user license agreement where you just automatically accept the terms of it. Or the user clicks "Submit" on your contact form without a thought about whether an attorney-client relationship is being established or whether they are relying to their detriment to some legal information in your blog.

Website visitors seldom navigate to the disclaimer page because that information has nothing to do with why they are on your website in the first place: to hire a lawyer for their legal issue. If they do navigate to our disclaimer, maybe they don't understand it, or maybe they don't read all of it, or whatever the case may be, the disclaimer may not in practical effect accomplish what we want it to accomplish.

This possible pointlessness notwithstanding, the reason the disclaimer is still important is that it tells the licensing authority in your State that we're doing our best, we're trying to manage users' expectations, and that we're in full compliance with recommended or prescribed local rules. We can't do more, nor can we be expected to.

In sum, the disclaimer is important for those two reasons: First, naturally, to try to get people to try to understand what they're reading on our website - what it is and what it isn't. Second, to make sure that the licensing authority (and our errors and omissions insurer) is satisfied with what we've published in our ecosystem.

Links to other websites

In the course of your ecosystem development, almost certainly at some point, you'll be linking to other websites from your website, social media and blog.

There is no Model Rule on point, nor any formal opinions that I've found, that speak to whether a website visitor may be mislead into thinking that a link to another law firm from your resources page or social media is a recommendation or referral to that law firm.

Nonetheless, it's worthwhile to include in your disclaimer that links to other law firms are not referrals or recommendations. This further helps us avoid liability for negligent referrals.

On this point, we want to manage two issues:

First, we want to make sure that people understand that when you're linking to another web site that the link is not a referral or recommendation.

Second, we want to make sure that your website visitor who navigates through that link understands that you are not responsible for the content of that website, it's accuracy, whether it's legal information or legal advice and whether it has the appropriate disclaimers in place.

You want to make sure that your disclaimer makes it clear to people that when you are linking out to other websites, whether that link is on your website itself, or whether it's on your social media, or through some other channel in your Ecosystem, that merely providing the link is not a referral and that you are not responsible for the content on the other side of that link.

If you have a resources page on your website that is dedicated to links to colleagues and/or other legal service providers, it would be a good idea to include this specific disclaimer on that page.

It gets problematic in the case of peer endorsements. For instance, we may *"highly recommend [lawyer's name] for your personal injury matters,"* in our social media, or websites like Avvo and LinkedIn. I have concerns about how to convince legal consumers that a peer endorsement is not a referral or recommendation, if indeed it is not.

Social Media

When you're putting content out in your social media, the normal Rules of 7.1 apply. That part, I think, is pretty obvious. If we're making statements in our social media that may be perceived by our local licensing authority as a testimonial or as what could be perceived as a guarantee of a case result ("I just got this tremendous case result – 6 Million dollars for this brain injury!"), there is a question as to whether required disclaimers should be in your social media, and strictly speaking, I think they should be.

It seems clear to me that if a personal injury law firm has a statement in its social media to the effect of "No fees unless we win," the qualifying statement about costs would need to be in there as well, in the States that require the qualifier.

There are some States that require the word, "Advertisement," if a particular social media post is viewed by the authorities as a communication advertising your legal services.

There have been cases where lawyers have been disciplined, and even disbarred, for certain activities in social media. One example was a lawyer in Louisiana, who, through social media, tried to get his local community to petition a couple of judges to influence their decision in a case. That lawyer got disbarred.

Another lawyer received a five-year suspension for having his plaintiff clean up his social media profile during the course of a wrongful death case of his spouse. In that case, the plaintiff had pictures of himself in his Facebook timeline that undercut their argument that the plaintiff was grieving.

There is another instance where (and this is more of advice to a client than to a lawyer themselves using social media) the daughter of a successful plaintiff posted in her social media a statement about how the defendant was paying for her trip to Europe. It was found that her post violated the confidentiality terms of the settlement agreement and her parents had to give the money back.

Another example involves civil defense lawyers who had their paralegal to "friend" a plaintiff to try to get information about the plaintiff's injuries. As of this writing, we don't know what is happening with that yet, but the New Jersey Supreme Court is deciding whether they want to discipline those attorneys.

And as a last example, a lawyer in Des Moines, Iowa, was found to have tainted the jury pool through hearsay that she put up on her social media and the judge ordered that the trial be delayed.

Solicitation

Rule 7.3 describes the ways in which you may and may not reach out to prospective clients for purposes of getting them to hire you for their legal matter. What's interesting about solicitation under the Model Rules of Profession Conduct, is how little is prohibited and how much is otherwise permitted.

I'm going to go through the prohibitions, keeping in mind that everything that is not a prohibition is, by implication, allowed. Again, please research your local rules.

Rule 7.3(a) says,

> *A lawyer shall not in person, live telephone, or real time electronic content, solicit professional employment."*

So, what does "in person, live telephone, real time electronic content" mean? If you are face-to-face or if on the phone with someone whom you'd like to have as a client, and that person is not at the moment started a conversation with you about legal representation, you cannot say "I see that you're badly injured there and it sounds to me like there's some liability and insurance, and we can turn your injury into cash, so you should hire us." You can't do that, *except* towards certain categories of people.

What is real time electronic content? In Ohio, it was determined that an exchange in a chatroom is considered real time communication, but that email and "texting" are not. A chat session from your website would likely be viewed as "real time electronic contact."

It's still permitted to engage in real-time solicitation towards certain categories of people. If that person is a lawyer, friend, relative or former client, you may invite them to hire you.

However, there is a qualification on that: even if they are in one of the categories of people you can solicit in real time, you still can't use real-time communication if the person you're approaching has made it clear that they don't want to be solicited. If they've made it clear that they have no desire to hire you, you can't do it.

You also can't use methods that are described in 7.3 as *"coercion, duress, or harassment."* So, if you're approaching someone at a party or you're on the phone and it's unsolicited, and they are a relative or a friend, former client or another lawyer, the solicitation is permitted unless you're using coercion, duress, or harassment. Then it's prohibited, That seems obvious enough, but curiously, the ABA felt there was a need to be explicit about it in the Model Rules.

Solicitation Using "Advertising Material"

Many States have the requirement that every written, recorded, or electronic communication from a lawyer soliciting professional employment shall include the words "Advertising Material" on the outside envelope and at the beginning and ending of any recorded or electronic communication.

So, if you are reaching out to somebody unsolicited to have them retain you, and it's not in real time, in many States you have to have the words "advertising material" at the beginning and at the end of your communication.

Unencrypted Email and the Attorney-Client Privilege

With respect to unencrypted email and our responsibilities as they relate to the Attorney-Client privilege, there are two issues to consider. One is the instance of just the usage of unencrypted email. We know that email is easy enough to intercept if someone knows what they're doing and have enough motivation.

The second issue is misdirected e-mail. Sometimes lawyers mistakenly send attorney-client privileged material to the wrong person.

To deal briefly with the usage of unencrypted email to transmit privileged material, the ABA issued Formal Ethics Opinion 99-413 that spoke to this particular issue. The ABA concluded that it did not violate the attorney-client privilege to use unencrypted email to send sensitive material back and forth between clients, co-counsel, etc. because there was a reasonable expectation of privacy when sending information by email.

Besides having a very positive practical impact on the practice of law, it makes sense. In the olden days, the risk of interception of regular, paper mail was probably as great or greater than it is in the digital world of sending and receiving e-mails through unencrypted routers. Especially when one compares the sheer volume of millions of paper letters to the tens of billions of daily emails.

However, in 2017, the ABA updated its position on this issue in Formal Ethics Opinion 477.[45] It states that lawyers must take reasonable efforts to ensure that communications with clients are secure and not subject to inadvertent or unauthorized security breaches.

The opinion offers seven considerations for guidance, including understanding:

    1.   The nature of the threat.

2. How client confidential info is transmitted and stored.

3. The use of reasonable electronic security measures.

4. How electronic communications should be protected.

5. The need to label client information as privileged and confidential.

6. The need to train lawyers and non-lawyer assistants in technology and cybersecurity.

7. The need to conduct due diligence on vendors who provide technology services.

The opinion also briefly notes that attorneys should inform their clients about risks inherent when transmitting "highly sensitive confidential client information."

The second issue is when you get an email accidentally from opposing counsel and there is an attachment, and that attachment may or may not include attorney-client privileged information.

Under Model Rule 4.4(b), relating to the respect for rights of third persons, a lawyer who receives a document from opposing counsel relating to the representation of the lawyer's client, that they knew or should have known was inadvertently sent, shall promptly notify the sender.

The interesting thing about the Model Rules in this instance is, in a comment to that rule, they leave open the question whether the privilege status of the document or the electronic stored information has been waived. This is curious because in my mind, I don't see how it could reasonably be argued under these circumstances that the attorney-client privilege was compromised.

As I see it, and maybe your State has spoken to this and has concluded so, that since the client owns the attorney-client privilege, that attorney-client privilege hasn't been compromised through the accidental disclosure of this document, especially in light of the fact that the recipient isn't supposed to open the sensitive attachment.

If your State has concluded under this scenario that the attorney-client privilege has been compromised, then the lawyer who sent the privileged document is in a great deal of trouble.

Eliciting reviews

Eliciting positive reviews is an important part of your Ecosystem development. The practice of getting clients to leave positive public feedback is not by itself a prohibited activity from an ethics standpoint.

That said, there are a few issues to keep in mind when we are asking former clients to leave good reviews for us.

First, you cannot have people who are not former clients leave fabricated reviews for you. This would fall squarely within the "false" communications prohibition of Rule 7.1.

Second, when we elicit reviews from satisfied clients, we have to make sure that we are not too specific in what we want them to say. Rule 8.4(a) says

> *"It is misconduct to violate or attempt to violate the rules of professional conduct by assisting or inducing another to do so."*

This is how Rule 8.4 would apply in this context. Under Rule 7.1, we can't describe ourselves in any way that is "false or misleading." We cover earlier in this chapter that there are many restrictions on attorney communications based upon what your local authorities have decided may be "misleading" to a legal consumer. For example, many States have restrictions on the use of a variety of superlatives, like "great" or "specialist."

Consequently, we cannot elicit a review from someone and ask them to use prohibited superlatives or to say anything else that would be "false or misleading" if we were to say it ourselves.

Satisfied clients may say on their own initiative anything they want, regardless of how false, misleading or non-verifiable it is. You cannot control what others write about you, positive or negative. Just don't be specific about what you want them to write.

Miscellaneous required disclaimers

This section covers how some States have modified the Model Rules as it relates to what we have discussed in this chapter. Additionally, we note a few disclaimers that are required for all attorneys who practice in certain areas of law.

IRS Circular 230:

The following disclaimer is required for tax lawyers:

> *To ensure compliance with requirements imposed by the IRS in Circular 230, we inform you that, unless*

expressly stated otherwise in this communication (including attachments), any tax advice contained in this communication is not intended or written to be used, and cannot be used, for the purpose of:

(i) avoiding penalties under the Internal Revenue Code or

(ii) promoting, marketing or recommending to another party any transaction or other matter addressed herein.

Bankruptcy Disclaimer

If you are a bankruptcy lawyer, you'll need this disclaimer:[46]

We are a debt relief agency. We help people file for bankruptcy relief under the Bankruptcy Code.

Immigration Law Disclaimer (California only)

If you are an immigration lawyer in California, Business and Professions Code Section 6157.5(a) requires the following disclaimer:

(a) All advertisements published, distributed, or broadcasted by or on behalf of a member seeking professional employment for the member in providing services relating to immigration or naturalization shall include a statement that he or she is an active member of the State Bar, licensed to practice law in this state. If the advertisement seeks employment for a law firm or law corporation employing more than one attorney, the advertisement shall include a statement that all the services relating to immigration and naturalization provided by the firm or corporation shall be provided by an active member of the State Bar or by a person under the supervision of an active member of the State Bar.

Contingency fees disclaimers

Many states require that if you have the statement on your website that you handle cases on a contingency fee basis, then you must also disclose who will be liable for court costs and other expenses related to the case. If you take cases on a contingency fee basis, you should check to see what your local rules say on this point. The following is what I have found in my research:

Arizona Rule 7.2(d)(1)

> *(d) Every advertisement (including advertisement by written solicitation) that contains information about the lawyer's fees shall be subject to the following requirements:*

> *(1) advertisements and written solicitations indicating that the charging of a fee is the client will be liable for expenses regardless of outcome unless the repayment of such is contingent upon the outcome of the matter and (B) whether the percentage fee will be computed before expenses are deducted from the recovery.*

California Rule 1-400(E)(14)

> *(14) A "communication" which states or implies "no fee without recovery" unless such communication also expressly discloses whether or not the client will be liable for costs.*

> *(d) A statement that a member offers representation on a contingent basis unless the statement also advises whether a client will be held responsible for any costs advanced by the member when no recovery is obtained on behalf of the client. If the client will not be held responsible for costs, no disclosure is required.*

Colorado Rule 7.1 (d)

(d) Any communication that states or implies the client does not have to pay a fee if there is no recovery shall also disclose that the client may be liable for costs. This provision does not apply to communications that only state that contingent or percentage fee arrangements are available, or that only state the initial consultation is free.

Connecticut Rule 7.2 (f)

(f) Every advertisement and written communication that contains information about the lawyer's fee, including those indicating that the charging of a fee is contingent on outcome, or that no fee will be charged in the absence of a recovery, or that the fee will be a percentage of the recovery, shall disclose whether and to what extent the client will be responsible for any court costs and expenses of litigation. The disclosure concerning court costs and expenses of litigation shall be in the same print size and type as the information regarding the lawyer's fee and, if broadcast, shall appear for the same duration as the information regarding the lawyer's fee. If the information regarding the fee is spoken, the disclosure concerning court costs and expenses of litigation shall also be spoken.

Florida Rule 4-7.2 (c)(7)

Every advertisement and unsolicited written communication that contains information about the lawyer's fee, including those that indicate no fee will be charged in the absence of a recovery, shall disclose whether the client will be liable for any expenses in addition to the fee.

Georgia Rule 7.1(a)(5) & (6)

(5) contains any information regarding contingent fees, and fails to conspicuously present the following disclaimer:

"Contingent attorneys' fees refer only to those fees charged by attorneys for their legal services. Such fees are not permitted in all types of cases. Court costs and other additional expenses of legal action usually must be paid by the client."

(6) contains the language "no fee unless you win or collect" or any similar phrase and fails to conspicuously present the following disclaimer:

"No fee unless you win or collect" (or insert the similar language used in the communication) refers only to fees charged by the attorney. Court costs and other additional expenses of legal action usually must be paid by the client. Contingent fees are not permitted in all types of cases.

Indiana Rule 7.2(b)

The following constitute examples of permissible areas in which a lawyer may advertise: (19)(C) contingent fee rates provided that the statement discloses whether percentages are computed before or after deduction of costs.

Iowa Rule 32:7.2: (h)(1)

Fee information may be communicated to the public in the manner permitted by this rule, provided it is presented in a dignified style. (iii) contingent fee rates, subject to rule 32:1.5(c) and (d), provided that the statement discloses whether percentages are computed before or after deduction of costs and advises the public that, in the event of an adverse verdict or decision, the contingent fee litigant could be liable for court costs, expenses of investigation, expenses of medical examinations, and costs of obtaining and presenting evidence.

Kentucky SCR 3.130(7.04)

If the client is required to pay court costs and/or case expenses in addition to the attorney's fee, the advertisement shall state in all capital letters, "COURT COSTS AND CASE EXPENSES WILL BE THE RESPONSIBILITY OF THE CLIENT."

Louisiana Rule 7.1 (a)(viii)

Communications that state or indicate that no fee will be charged in the absence of recovery shall disclose that the client will be liable for certain expenses in addition to the fee, if such is the case.

Maryland Rule 7.2(e)

An advertisement or communication indicating that no fee will be charged in the absence of a recovery shall also disclose whether the client will be liable for any expenses.

Missouri Rule 4-7.1(k)

A communication is misleading if it: (k) states that legal services are available on a contingent or no-recovery-no-fee basis without stating conspicuously that the client may be responsible for costs or expenses, if that is the case.

Nevada Rule 7.2(e)

This Disclaimer appears to apply whether it is a contingency fee arrangement or otherwise.

"You may have to pay the opposing party's attorney fees and costs in the event of a loss."

New Mexico Rule 16-702(E)(3)

Lawyer advertisements or solicitations may contain information about fees for services as follows:

(3) contingent fee rates, or a statement to the effect that the charging of a fee is contingent on outcome or that the fee will be a percentage of recovery, provided that the statement discloses (a) whether percentages are computed before or after deduction of costs, and (b) specifically states that the client will bear the expenses incurred in the client's case regardless of outcome

Pennsylvania Rule 7.2(h)(1)

Advertisements that state or indicate that no fee shall be charged in the absence of recovery shall disclose that the client will be liable for certain expenses in addition to the fee, if such is the case.

Rhode Island Rule 7.2(e)

Lawyer advertising or written communications which indicate that no fee will be charged if no recovery, shall also state conspicuously if the client will be responsible for costs or expenses regardless of outcome.

South Carolina Rule 7.2(g)

Every advertisement that contains information about the lawyer's fee shall disclose whether the client will be liable for any expenses in addition to the fee and, if the fee will be a percentage of the recovery, whether the percentage will be computed before deducting the expenses.

South Dakota Rule 7.2(g)

Advertisements permitted under this Rule 7.2 may contain information about fees for services as follows:

(iii) that the charging of a fee is contingent on outcome or that the fee will be a percentage of the recovery, provided that the advertisement conspicuously discloses whether percentages are computed before or after deduction of costs, and only if it specifically and conspicuously states that the client will bear the expenses incurred in the client's representation, regardless of outcome, except as permitted by Rule 1.8(e).

Texas Rule 7.04(h)

If an advertisement in the public media by a lawyer or firm discloses the willingness or potential willingness of the lawyer or firm to render services on a contingent fee basis, the advertisement must state whether the client will be obligated to pay all or any portion of the court costs and, if a client may be liable for other expenses, this fact must be disclosed. If specific percentage fees or fee ranges of contingent fee work are disclosed in such advertisement, it must also disclose whether the percentage is computed before or after expenses are deducted from the recovery.

Other locally mandated disclaimers

Many states require that the word "advertisement" or "attorney advertising" be prominently featured in all of the law firm's communications, including its website.

Alabama Rule 7.2(e)

"No representation is made that the quality of the legal services to be performed is greater than the quality of legal services performed by other lawyers."

Florida Rule 4-7.6(b)

(b) Internet Presence. All World Wide Web sites and home pages accessed via the Internet that are controlled or sponsored by a lawyer or law firm and that contain information concerning the lawyer's or law firm's services:

(1) shall disclose all jurisdictions in which the lawyer or members of the law firm are licensed to practice law;

(2) shall disclose 1 or more bona fide office locations of the lawyer or law firm, in accordance with subdivision (a)(2) of rule 4-7.2; and

(3) are considered to be information provided upon request.

Kentucky SCR 3.130(7.25)

"THIS IS AN ADVERTISEMENT"

The Commission may require the statement "THIS IS AN ADVERTISEMENT" for any advertisement that may not be perceived as a quest for clients because of the format, manner of presentation or medium. If the statement is required, it shall be spoken in all audio advertisements at the end thereof and in all other advertisements, shall be in color and size print equal to the lawyer's or firm name and visually present for as long as the lawyer's or firm's name.

Mississippi Rule 7.4 (a)(2)

"FREE BACKGROUND INFORMATION AVAILABLE UPON REQUEST."

Missouri Rule 4-7.2(f)

"The choice of a lawyer is an important decision and should not be based solely upon advertisements."

New York Rule DR 2-101(f)

Every advertisement other than those appearing in a radio or television advertisement or in a directory, newspaper, magazine or other periodical (and any web sites related thereto), or made in person pursuant to DR 2-103 [1200.8] (A)(1), shall be labeled "Attorney Advertising" on the first page, or on the home page in the case of a web site. If the communication is in the form of a self-mailing brochure or postcard, the words "Attorney Advertising" shall appear therein. In the case of electronic mail, the subject line shall contain the notation "ATTORNEY ADVERTISINC."

Virginia Rule 7.2(a)(3)

(3) advertises specific or cumulative case results, without a disclaimer that (i) puts the case results in a context that is not misleading; (ii) states that case results depend upon a variety of factors unique to each case; and (iii) further states that case results do not guarantee or predict a similar result in any future case undertaken by the lawyer. The disclaimer shall precede the communication of the case results. When the communication is in writing, the disclaimer shall be in bold type face and uppercase letters in a font size that is at least as large as the largest text used to advertise the specific or cumulative case results and in the same color and against the same colored background as the text used to advertise the specific or cumulative case results.

Wyoming Rule 7.2(g)

(g) Except as permitted by Rule 7.4, advertisement containing information in addition to that set forth in Rule 7.2(c) shall contain the following disclaimer:

The Wyoming State Bar does not certify any lawyer as a specialist or expert. Anyone considering a lawyer should independently investigate the lawyer's credentials and ability, and not rely upon advertisements or self-proclaimed expertise.

The disclaimer must appear within the advertisement itself, or in the instance of a telephone or other directory, upon the same or the facing page as the advertisement appears. The disclaimer shall be in a type size at least as large as the smallest type size appearing in the advertisement.

Disclaimers relating to the use of the word "Specialist"

Many states have restrictions on the use of the word "specialist" when describing your law practice. In some states like California, it is an outright prohibition unless the attorney is certified as a specialist by the State Bar of California, which states it in this way in Rules of Professional Conduct Rule 1-400(D)(6):

(D) A communication or a solicitation (as defined herein) shall not:

(6) State that a member is a "certified specialist" unless the member holds a current certificate as a specialist issued by the Board of Legal Specialization, or any other entity accredited by the State Bar to designate specialists pursuant to standards adopted by the Board of Governors, and states the complete name of the entity which granted certification.

Alabama, Alaska, Arkansas, Delaware, Idaho, Iowa, Kansas, Maine, Montana, Nebraska, North Carolina, and Ohio have nearly identical language, as follows, in their versions of Rule 7.4(d):

> *(d) A lawyer shall not state or imply that a lawyer is certified as a specialist in a particular field of law, unless:*
>
> *(1) the lawyer has been certified as a specialist by an organization that has been approved by an appropriate state authority or that has been accredited by the American Bar Association; and*
>
> *(2) the name of the certifying organization is clearly identified in the communication.*

Colorado Rules Rule 7.4(e) & (f)

> *(d) A lawyer shall not state or imply that a lawyer is certified as a specialist in a particular field of law, unless:*
>
> *(1) the lawyer has been certified as a specialist by an organization that has been approved by an appropriate state authority or that has been accredited by the American Bar Association; and*
>
> *(2) the name of the certifying organization is clearly identified in the communication.*
>
> *(e) In any advertisement in which a lawyer affirmatively claims to be certified in any area of the law, such advertisement shall contain the following disclosure: "Colorado does not certify lawyers as specialists in any field." This disclaimer is not required where the information concerning the lawyer's services is contained in a law list, law directory or a publication intended primarily for use of the legal profession.*

Florida Rule 4-7.2 (c)(6)(A)

(A) Florida Bar Certified Lawyers. A lawyer who complies with the Florida certification plan as set forth in chapter 6, Rules Regulating The Florida Bar, may inform the public and other lawyers of the lawyer's certified areas of legal practice. Such communications should identify The Florida Bar as the certifying organization and may state that the lawyer is "certified," "board certified," a "specialist in (area of certification)," or an "expert in (area of certification)."

Hawaii Rule 7.4(c)

"The Supreme Court of Hawaii grants Hawaii certification only to lawyers in good standing who have successfully completed a specialty program accredited by the American Bar Association."

Illinois Rule 7.4(c)(2)

"The Supreme Court of Illinois does not recognize certifications of specialties in the practice of law and that the certificate, award or recognition is not a requirement to practice law in Illinois."

Indiana Rule 7.4(a)

Rule 7.4: (a)The lawyer shall not represent, either expressly or impliedly, that the lawyer's certification has been individually recognized by the Indiana Supreme Court or CLE, or by an entity other than the ICO.

Indiana Rules for Admission to the Bar and Discipline of Attorneys Rule 30 Section 6(a)

Rule 30 Section 6: (a) A lawyer who is certified under this rule may communicate the fact that the lawyer is certified by the ICO as a specialist in the area of law involved. The lawyer shall not represent, either expressly or impliedly, that the lawyer's certification has been individually recognized by the Indiana Supreme Court or CLE, or by an entity other than the ICO.

Kentucky SCR 3.130(7.40)(3)

A lawyer may communicate the fact that he or she has achieved a national certificate by an organization qualifying under Peel v. Attorney Registration and Disciplinary Commission of Illinois, 110 S.Ct. 2281 (1990), by clearly identifying the certification and the organization that has conferred the distinction, and such communication may occur only for so long as the lawyer remains so certified and in good standing with the organization.

Massachusetts Rule 7.4(b)

Lawyers who hold themselves out as "certified" in a particular service, field, or area of law must name the certifying organization and must state that the certifying organization is "a private organization, whose standards for certification are not regulated by the Commonwealth of Massachusetts," if that is the case, or, if the certifying organization is a governmental body, must name the governmental body.

Minnesota Rule 7.4(d)(2)

If the attorney is not certified as a specialist or if the certifying organization is not accredited by the Minnesota Board of Legal Certification, the communication shall clearly state that the attorney is not certified by any organization accredited by that Board, and in any advertising subject to Rule 7.2, this statement shall appear in the same sentence that communicates the certification.

Mississippi Rule 7.6(a)

Mississippi requires disclosure of the name of the certifying organization and the following disclaimer:

> *"There is no procedure in Mississippi for approving certifying or designating organizations and authorities."*

> *A lawyer may communicate the fact that he or she has been certified or designated in a field of law by a named organization or authority, but only if that certification or designation is granted by an organization or authority whose specialty certification or designation program is accredited by the American Bar Association. Notwithstanding the provisions of this Rule, a lawyer may communicate the fact that he is certified or designated in a particular field of law by a named, non-American Bar Association organization or authority, but must disclose such fact and further disclose that there is no procedure in Mississippi for approving certifying or designating organizations and authorities.*

Missouri Rule 4-7.4

> *A lawyer shall not state or imply that the lawyer is a specialist unless the communication contains a disclaimer that neither the Supreme Court of Missouri nor The Missouri Bar reviews or approves certifying organizations or specialist designations.*

Nevada Rule 7.4 (d)(5)

> *A lawyer certified as a specialist under this Rule may advertise the certification during such time as the lawyer's certification and the state bar's approval of the certifying organization are both in effect. Advertising by a lawyer regarding the lawyer's*

*certification under this Rule shall comply with Rules
7.1 and 7.2 and shall clearly identify the name of the
certifying organization.*

New Jersey Rules RPC 7.4(d)

*A lawyer may communicate that the lawyer has been
certified as a specialist or certified in a field of practice
only when the communication is not false or
misleading, states the name of the certifying
organization, and states that the certification has been
granted by the Supreme Court of New Jersey or by an
organization that has been approved by the American
Bar Association. If the certification has been granted
by an organization that has not been approved, or has
been denied approval, by the Supreme Court of New
Jersey or the American Bar Association, the absence
or denial of such approval shall be clearly identified in
each such communication by the lawyer.*

New Mexico Rule 16-704(D)

*[T]he statement is accompanied by a prominent
disclaimer that such certification does not constitute
recognition by the New Mexico Board of Legal
Specialization, unless the lawyer is also recognized by
the board as a specialist in that area of law or the
board does not recognize specialization in that area.*

New York Rule DR 2-105(c)

*(c)(1) A lawyer who is certified as a specialist in a
particular area of law or law practice by a private
organization approved for that purpose by the
American Bar Association may state the fact of
certification if, in conjunction therewith, the certifying
organization is identified and the following statement
is prominently made:*

"The [name of the private certifying organization] is not affiliated with any governmental authority. Certification is not a requirement for the practice of law in the State of New York and does not necessarily indicate greater competence than other attorneys experienced in this field of law."

(2) A lawyer who is certified as a specialist in a particular area of law or law practice by the authority having jurisdiction over specialization under the laws of another state or territory may state the fact of certification if, in conjunction therewith, the certifying state or territory is identified and the following statement is prominently made:

"Certification granted by the [identify state or territory] is not recognized by any governmental authority within the State of New York. Certification is not a requirement for the practice of law in the State of New York and does not necessarily indicate greater competence than other attorneys experienced in this field of law."

North Dakota Rule 7.4(c)

A lawyer may communicate the fact that the lawyer has been certified as a specialist in a field of law by a named organization, provided that the communication clearly states the name of the certifying organization and that there is no procedure in this jurisdiction for approving certifying organizations. The communication need not contain such a statement if the named organization has been accredited by the American Bar Association or the lawyer has successfully completed a certification program sponsored by a state bar association.

Oklahoma Rule 7.4(4)

A lawyer who is certified as a specialist in a particular field of law or law practice by the official licensing authority of another state in which the lawyer is licensed may communicate that fact, but only in accordance with all rules and requirements of such state's licensing authority, and provided that the lawyer also communicates that such certification is not recognized by the Supreme Court of the State of Oklahoma.

Rhode Island Rule 7.4(d)

(d) A lawyer shall not state or imply that a lawyer is certified as a specialist in a particular field of law, unless:

(1) the lawyer has been certified as a specialist by an organization that has been approved by an appropriate state authority or that has been accredited by the American Bar Association;

(2) the name of the certifying organization is clearly identified in the communication; and

(3) the lawyer also includes, as part of the same communication, the disclaimer that:

"The Rhode Island Supreme Court licenses all lawyers in the general practice of law. The court does not license or certify any lawyer as an expert or specialist in any particular field of practice."

South Dakota Rule 7.4(c)

A lawyer shall not state or imply that the lawyer is a specialist except as follows:

(c) If a lawyer or firm practices in only certain fields and desires to advertise such limitations in the yellow pages of the telephone directory any such advertising

must be accompanied by the following disclaimer appearing in a prominent and conspicuous manner in such advertising or on the same page as the advertising:

(1) Such certification is granted by an organization which has been approved by the appropriate regulatory authority to grant such certification; or

(2) Such certification is granted by an organization that has not yet been approved by, or has been denied the approval available from the appropriate regulatory authority, and the absence or denial of approval is clearly stated in the communication, and in any advertising subject to Rule 7.2, such statement appears in the same sentence that communicates the certification.

Tennessee Rule 7.4(d)

(d) A lawyer who has been certified as a specialist in a field of law by the Tennessee Commission on Continuing Legal Education and Specialization may state that the lawyer "is certified as a specialist in [field of law] by the Tennessee Commission on C.L.E. and Specialization." A lawyer so certified may also state that the lawyer is certified as a specialist in that field of law by an organization recognized or accredited by the Tennessee Commission on Continuing Legal Education and Specialization as complying with its requirements, provided the statement is made in the following format: "[Lawyer] is certified as a specialist in [field of law] by [organization]."

Tennessee Formal Ethics Opinion 2001-F-144(b)

Therefore lawyers listing areas of practice on the Internet, including law directories or other Web sites available to the general public should comply with the certification of specialization disclosure requirements of DR 2-101(C). The specific disclosure language of DR 2-101(C) may be included or, in the alternative compliance is assured if the initial screen for each lawyer includes the following precise explanation displayed in a prominent manner.

Certifications of Specialization are available to Tennessee lawyers in all areas of practice relating to or included in the areas of Civil Trial, Criminal Trial, Business Bankruptcy, Consumer Bankruptcy, Creditor's Rights, Medical Malpractice, Legal Malpractice, Accounting Malpractice, Elder Law, Estate Planning and Family Law. Listing of related or included practice areas herein does not constitute or imply a representation of certification of specialization.

Texas Rule 7.04(b)

A lawyer who advertises in the public media: (2) shall not include a statement that the lawyer has been certified or designated by an organization as possessing special competence or a statement that the lawyer is a member of an organization the name of which implies that its members possess special competence, except that:

(ii) a lawyer who is a member of an organization the name of which implies that its members possess special competence, or who has been certified or designated by an organization as possessing special competence, may include a factually accurate statement of such membership or may include a factually accurate statement, "Certified [area of specialization] [name of certifying organization]," but such statements may be made only if that organization has been accredited by the Texas Board of Legal Specialization as a bona

fide organization that admits to membership or grants certification only on the basis of objective, exacting, publicly available standards (including high standards of individual character, conduct, and reputation) that are reasonably relevant to the special training or special competence that is implied and that are in excess of the level of training and competence generally required for admission to the Bar.

Utah Rule 7.4(d)

A lawyer shall not state or imply that a lawyer is certified as a specialist in a particular field of law, unless:

(d)(1) the lawyer has been certified as a specialist by an organization that has been approved by an appropriate state authority or that has been accredited by the American Bar Association; and

(d)(2) the name of the certifying organization is clearly identified in the communication.

Vermont Rule 7.4(c)

(c) a lawyer may communicate the fact that the lawyer has been certified as a specialist in a field of law by a named organization, provided that the communication clearly states that there is no procedure in Vermont for approving certifying organizations. If, however, the named organization has been accredited by the American Bar Association to certify lawyers as specialists in a particular field of law, the communication need not contain such a statement.

Virginia Rule 7.4(c) & (d)

(c) A lawyer who has been certified by the Supreme Court of Virginia as a specialist in some capacity may

use the designation of being so certified, e. g., "certified mediator" or a substantially similar designation;

(d) A lawyer may communicate the fact that the lawyer has been certified as a specialist in a field of law by a named organization, provided that the communication clearly states that there is no procedure in the Commonwealth of Virginia for approving certifying organizations.

Washington Rules Rule 7.4(d)

(d) A lawyer shall not state or imply that a lawyer is a specialist in a particular field of law, except upon issuance of an identifying certificate, award, or recognition by a group, organization, or association, a lawyer may use the terms "certified", " specialist", "expert", or any other similar term to describe his or her qualifications as a lawyer or his or her qualifications in any subspecialty of the law. If the terms are used to identify any certificate, award, or recognition by any group, organization, or association, the reference must:

(1) be truthful and verifiable and otherwise comply with Rule 7.1;

(2) identify the certifying group, organization, or association; and

(3) state that the Supreme Court of Washington does not recognize the certification of specialties in the practice of law and that the certificate, award, or recognition is not a requirement to practice law in the state of Washington.

Wisconsin SCR 20:7.4(d)

A lawyer shall not state or imply that a lawyer is certified as a specialist in a particular field of law, unless:

(1) the lawyer has been certified as a specialist by an organization that has been approved by an appropriate state authority or that has been accredited by the American Bar Association; and (2) the name of the certifying organization is clearly identified in the communication.

Wyoming Rule 7.4(d)

A lawyer shall not state or imply that the lawyer is certified as a specialist in a particular field of law, unless:

(1) the lawyer has been certified as a specialist by an organization that has been approved by the Wyoming State Bar; and

(2) the name of the certifying organization is clearly identified in the communication.

Please check your local rules for restrictions on describing your expertise and specialization in your practice areas.

Disclaimers relating to the use of testimonials and comparisons with other law firms

Many states have restrictions or prohibitions on the use of testimonials on a law firm website in their case law and formal opinions, and some states have specific rules on point.

New Jersey RPC 7.1(a)(3)

"No aspect of this advertisement has been approved by the Supreme Court of New Jersey."

(a) A lawyer shall not make false or misleading communications about the lawyer, the lawyer's services, or any matter in which the lawyer has or seeks a professional involvement. A communication is false or misleading if it:

(3) compares the lawyer's services with other lawyers' services, unless (i) the name of the comparing organization is stated, (ii) the basis for the comparison can be substantiated, and (iii) the communication includes the following disclaimer in a readily discernable manner: "No aspect of this advertisement has been approved by the Supreme Court of New Jersey."

New York Rules 7.1(d)(3) and (e)(3)

(d) An advertisement that complies with paragraph (e) may contain the following:

(3) testimonials or endorsements of clients, where not prohibited by paragraph (c)(1), and of former clients

(e) It is permissible to provide the information set forth in paragraph (d) provided:

(3) it is accompanied by the following disclaimer: "Prior results do not guarantee a similar outcome."

New York State Bar Association Professional Ethics Comm., Op. 834

"Prior results do not guarantee a similar outcome."

Privacy Policies

The California Online Privacy Protection Act of 2003 states that any commercial website or online service that collects personal information from a California resident must have a privacy policy.

Even if you're practicing law in one of the other 49 States, California sees the privacy policy as mandatory for any commercial website in the U.S. if the website *"collects and maintains personally identifiable information from a consumer residing in California who uses or visits"* the online service.

Google has a privacy policy requirement as well. If you're a Google advertiser, you need a privacy policy.

Regardless of any legal requirement, it's good to have one. The best reason to have a privacy policy on your website is because it makes your website more comfortable to its visitors. A privacy policy demonstrates that you're concerned about their privacy. There is currently concern among consumers about data sharing and the extent to which the government and Google collect information and your privacy policy will make your site visitors feel a little better about your website and your explicit limited use of collected information.

Here's the heart of the message you want to convey: *"We're not going to share your information with anyone. We care about your privacy."*

Here are recommended elements of a privacy policy, and there is a complete generic privacy policy for you to use in Appendix C if you'd like.

- Include a conspicuous link in the homepage with the words "Privacy Policy" in it.

- Indicate what you do with the information.

- Specify your security measures (e.g., encryption of the email correspondence).

- Disclose visitor tracking through Analytics and cookies.

- Include a "Delete" policy.

- Make it clear that you are not responsible for the privacy policies of other websites to which you link.

- Include contact information for questions.

- Offer an "opt-out of future correspondence" link.

Table of Figures

350

Appendix A – A Quick Guide to SEO

This Appendix is intended to serve as a brief do-it-yourself guide to search engine optimization (SEO) to help you get your website as visible as possible in Google without investing a lot of money on the process. It's a good idea to outsource SEO to a competent provider if you have the capital, but for the cash-strapped law firm, this guide will get you started.

Google told us that the top two ranking factors in its algorithm are links to your website (off-page SEO) and content (on-page SEO). So for purposes of this guide, SEO is divided into these two parts: on-page SEO and off-page SEO. We'll deal with on-page SEO first.

I. On-Page SEO

On-page SEO refers to the page-by-page refinement (and continuing refinement as your content continues to expand) of your existing website content so that's easy for Google to index and to understand for what searches your pages are relevant.

If your website is in WordPress, an important first step is to get a plug-in that can help you evaluate how optimized your page is and what you need to improve the page. My recommendation is Yoast or All-in-One-SEO. Both are excellent and free of charge.

As a preliminary matter, decide what phrase or phrases for which you would like the page to be perceived as relevant by Google. These are known as your "keywords."

1. Get your pre-selected keywords into your page's "Meta Data."

The term "Meta Data" refers to the content in the source of your website's pages that people don't see on the site but Google does. "Meta tags" are the code that hold your meta data.

For the most part, there are only two meta tags that you need to concern yourself with: "Title" and "Description". A third meta tag, "Keywords," is safe to ignore because no major search engine looks at them anymore.

A. Title tag

Your keywords should be the first part of your title tag. In the following example, we optimized this page for "Isla Vista Criminal Lawyer" and several related phrases

```
<html xmlns="http://www.w3.org/1999/xhtml">
<head>
<meta http-equiv="Content-Type" content="text/html; charset=UTF-8" />
<title>Isla Vista Criminal Lawyer - Law Offices of William C. Makler,
P.C.</title>

<meta name="description" content="Information about DUI and criminal
charges, free consultation with a Santa Barbara Criminal & DUI Defense
Attorney." />
<meta name="google-site-verification"
content="CCMTQnvtsfdgdS0rCad5xPOQBGZaT_TxY14FDkBp6zc" />
<meta name="keywords" content="Santa Barbara criminal law
firm,criminal,checkpoint,dmv,battery,crime,DUI, Drunk
Driving,Drunk,charges,police,jail,DMV,arrest,license,California,lawyer,
drugs,intoxication,defense,attorney,Driving,23152, citation,theft" />
```

Simple keyword stuffing is not advised because the Title tag is the link in the search results, as seen here for the search for "Isla Vista Criminal Lawyer:"

Isla Vista Criminal Lawyer - Law Offices of William C. Makler, P.C.
www.ivlawyer.com/ ▾
Information about DUI and criminal charges, free consultation with a Santa Barbara Criminal & DUI Defense Attorney

It is recommended to keep your Title for each page no longer than about 60 characters because that's roughly the number of characters Google displays in it's search results.

B. Description tag

The Description tag is not thought to be a ranking factor but your keywords can be in there as well if possible because Google bolds the matching words in its search results snippet. Here is an example of a description tag from the same page we used in the example above:

```
<html xmlns="http://www.w3.org/1999/xhtml">
<head>
<meta http-equiv="Content-Type" content="text/html; charset=UTF-8" />
<title>Isla Vista Criminal Lawyer - Law Offices of William C. Makler,
P.C.</title>
<meta name="description" content="Information about DUI and criminal
charges, free consultation with a Santa Barbara Criminal & DUI Defense
Attorney." />
<meta name="google-site-verification"
content="CCMTQnvtsfdgdSOrCad5xPOQBGZaT_TxY14FDkBp6zc" />
<meta name="keywords" content="Santa Barbara criminal law
firm,criminal,checkpoint,dmv,battery,crime,DUI, Drunk
Driving,Drunk,charges,police,jail,DMV,arrest,license,California,lawyer,
drugs,intoxication,defense,attorney,Driving,23152, citation,theft" />
```

The description tag's primary purpose is to convey a message that will cause Google users to click on your link when they see it in the search results. Notice in this same snippet from above how the description tag makes up the body of the search result:

2. Work your keywords into your headings if you can.

Headings are displayed in your main content for your website visitors and headings serve to break up your content into skimmable chunks so that people can get to the page content they want as easily as possible. Because we're writing primarily for people, not Google, we want to make sure that we don't overdo it on the keyword stuffing.

Headings are in tiers: the highest level of heading is H1 and is the main heading of your page, the second highest is H2, and so on. You can have as many tiers of headings as you need, but 3 or 4 is usually the limit needed for the content of most pages.

For purposes of SEO, Google views H1 heading as the most important, H2s as second most, etc. Only have one H1.

Below is an example of what your headings look like in the source code of your website:

```
<h1>Do You Need an Isla Vista Criminal Lawyer?</h1>
    <p><strong>Call now at 805.892.4922 </strong></p>
    <p><strong>Aggressive Criminal Defense Against MIP, DUI, Drunk In
Public & Other Charges </strong></p>
    <p>If you have been arrested (or otherwise cited for any law
violation) in Isla Vista or on the UCSB campus, you need to speak to a
lawyer right away. The Law Offices of William C. Makler, P. C. offers a
free, immediate and confidential consultation to any person in these
circumstances. </p>
    <h2>Don't go to court without an experienced criminal defense lawyer
by your side.</h2>
    <p>Don't just assume that it's no big deal and/or that you will be
treated fairly following an arrest in Isla Vista. If you care about your
future you owe it to yourself, and your family (perhaps), to carefully
consider what may be the impact on you (especially in the long-term) of
incurring a criminal conviction, license suspension, etc. MIPs, DUIs,
Public Intoxications, Fake ID's, Furnishing Alcohol to Minors, Possession
of Marijuana and matters more serious, carry severe, yet often avoidable,
consequences. Call 805-892-4922 (or send a message at right) to discuss
your options with a qualified lawyer today!</p>
    <h3>Have questions about your arrest?</h3>
    <p>Students arrested in I.V. (and their loved ones) often have
questions about the criminal justice process and possible repercussions.
Check out our <A CLASS="undefined" HREF="ivlegalfaq.html" TARGET="_self"
MCE_REAL_HREF="page2.html" >FAQ</A> to find answers to the most common of
these questions.</p>
```

Notice how we were able to work one of our target keywords "Isla Vista Criminal Lawyer" into the H1 heading. In the second level heading, H2, we added "criminal defense lawyer," not trying to force the target phrase "Isla Vista Criminal Attorney" into the heading for fear of the page looking to the website visitor as shamelessly written for Google, not them.

3. Make sure the content is useful and relevant to your keywords.

This part seems obvious but we want content that is of high-quality that is on topic. We want people to stay on your page once they get there, and Google does too because they want to serve up good content.

Without obviously keyword stuffing, try to get your target keywords subtly into the content if possible.

It has been found that pages of 1,000 words and longer rank higher often, but shorter pages rank well too. I'd recommend not spending too much time doing word-counts and adding paragraphs to exceed the 1,000 word threshold, but I mention it because you want to keep it in mind in case, when optimizing a page, you think of more to say on the topic that may be of interest to the visitor.

4. Add schema mark-up if you have time.

Schema mark-up labels your contact information to help Google understand what it is. So to tell Google that you are a Local Business with the name "Johnson & Smith Law Firm," you enclose your name information in a tag like this:

<div itemscope itemtype="http://schema.org/LocalBusiness"> <h2 itemprop="name">Johnson & Smith Law Firm </h2>

A full example of this particular schema can be found in Appendix G, following.

Now that we have the on-page refinement of each current page complete, make sure you make it a practice to optimize every page you add to the website later, including blog posts.

II. Off-page SEO

Off-page SEO refers to what you do on the web off your website to help Google see your pages as important information sources for particular searches. These are known as "trust factors" – that is to say, links and references to your website and law firm cause Google to trust it more as a good resource for Google users.

Much of your ecosystem development is part of off-page SEO, with your law firm's social media,

YouTube channel and other online properties serving as trust factors for Google.

Since links continue to be the number one ranking factor, we need to get some. Not all links are of equal value. A single link from an important page on the American Bar Association website or from a federal government website can be worth 100,000 links from other attorneys' websites.

An easy way to get links are through directory listings, many of which are free and some of which are of significant value. In the SEO community, these are often referred to as "structured citations" so that SEO providers can charge more for the simple, and often automated, service.

A list of directories can be found in Appendix F, following.

Here are the steps to create your own "structured citations:"

1. Choose your "NAP"

First, settle upon a name-address-phone number convention. This is known in the SEO world as your "NAP." Your NAP should be absolutely consistent across all directories (or as much as possible considering your in-house staff resources).

When choosing your NAP, it is sometimes recommended that you look up the US Postal Service convention for your address and use that.

For example, let's say your address from the USPS is as follows:

Mary Johnson, Esq.

Johnson & Smith Law Firm, P.C.

1234 Main Street, Ste 200

San Francisco, CA 94102-1234

And your phone number is "(415) 555-1212."

This will be your NAP.

When we're talking about absolute consistency, we mean absolute consistency. Use "Ste" for your suite, not "Suite" or "#". Always use the nine-digit zip code and always put your telephone area code in parenthesis (if this is the convention you've selected for your firm – if you display your phone number in a different way, like "415.555.1212" then always do it that way).

2. Choose a directory and check to see if you already have a listing in there.

If you have found that your firm already has a listing in the directory, see if the listing conforms to your NAP. If it doesn't, claim this listing by whatever means the directory offers (this is not always easy) so that you can make it conform. Do not create a second listing.

If you are in the directory more than once, claim all of the listings and delete all but one of them.

Final note:

SEO is a bottomless pit of work and this is only the beginning of what you can do. Whole books have been dedicated to the topic but I'd be hard-pressed to name one that I could recommend.

A few examples of what also can be done but are beyond the scope of this short guide are as follows:

- Keyword-rich file names for your pages (for example, www.johnsonsmithlawfirm/practice-areas/auto-accidents);

- ALT tags and captions for images;

- Press releases and guest blogging;

- Internal linking between your existing page content;

- Linking out to useful, trustworthy sites;

- Adding your blog to syndication and feed services;

- Recycling your content in various formats like a slideshow at slideshare or a pdf at Pinterest;

- And the list goes on.

I hope this helps.

Good luck.

Appendix B – Privacy Policy

Privacy Policy

[LAW FIRM] has created this statement to demonstrate its firm commitment to your privacy. This Privacy Policy describes the information we collect about you and what will happen to that information. Questions regarding this statement should be directed to [LAW FIRM] at info@[LAW FIRM].com.

Information About You

When you make contact with [LAW FIRM] through this website, we ask you to provide information about your legal problem. In addition, we request that you provide your name, telephone, and email address.

This information that you provide is held in the strictest confidence. The information that you provide will be reviewed by [LAW FIRM] for purposes of responding to your inquiry.

It is [LAW FIRM]'s policy to respect the privacy of its website visitors. Except as described above, under no circumstances will [LAW FIRM] disclose information provided by you to any individual, advertiser, vendor, or any other entity without your express, prior written consent.

If you send correspondence to [LAW FIRM], such as emails or letters, we may collect such information into a file specific to you. We may use information in the file we maintain about you and other information we obtain from your current and past use of the website to assess problems or complaints.

Future Correspondence From [LAW FIRM]

If you would like to opt out of receiving future correspondence from the law firm, please write to us at the email address above with the word "Unsubscribe" in the subject line of your email.

Security

We take precautions internally to protect your information. While we make every effort to keep your data as secure as possible, when you submit information via the website, your information is sent through the Internet by unencrypted email, so the transmission of sensitive, confidential, or privileged information through this website should be avoided.

IP Addresses

[LAW FIRM] may on occasion log IP addresses for systems administration purposes. Your IP address may be used to gather broad demographic information, but we would not use IP addresses to monitor your behavior on this site or elsewhere.

[IF YOU USE COOKIES, ADD THIS]

Cookies

A cookie is a small piece of text sent to your browser by a website you visit. It helps the website to remember information about your visit, like your preferred language and other settings. In addition, [LAW FIRM] may use "cookies" for advertising.

Delete Policy

[LAW FIRM] does not offer users a means by which to delete personal information provided to them.

Links to Other Sites

This site may contain links to other web sites. [LAW FIRM] is not responsible for the content or the privacy policies of websites to which it links.

Appendix C – Disclaimer

[DISCLAIMER ABOUT THIS DISCLAIMER: Please note that every state is different, and this disclaimer may or may not satisfy all of the requirements of your local rules.]

Disclaimer

No attorney-client relationship is formed with this firm until both [LAW FIRM] and our client sign a completed legal services agreement. Do not send us any confidential information or documents through the [LAW FIRM] website.

The materials provided on this website and in our social media content, including but not limited to Facebook, Twitter, LinkedIn, and Google+, are for informational purposes only and are not guaranteed to be correct, complete, or current and should not be relied on as legal advice. Every case is different and your case or claim may not bring results similar to those described in this website or in our social media. You should consult a lawyer if you need help with legal matters. No attorney-client relationship is or can be established by reviewing information on our website, social media, or by communicating with our firm by email or through social media messaging.

In our social media and on this website we link to content on other websites. Our law firm is not responsible for the content of other websites to which we link, and the content of those websites is not guaranteed to be correct, complete, or current and should not be relied on as legal advice.

Through our social media platforms we connect with many other businesses, organizations, individuals, and other entities through "Likes," "Followers," "Plus-ones," and the like. We are not responsible for the content, views, or opinions of those to whom we are connected, and the content of those websites and social media accounts are not guaranteed to be correct, complete, or current and should not be relied on as legal advice. Further, our connection to another entity through our social media is in no way to be understood as a referral to or recommendation of that other entity.

While we would be pleased to communicate with you by email or social media messaging, we cannot represent you until we know that doing so will not create a conflict of interest. Also, if you communicate with us by email or through social media in connection with a matter for which we do not already represent you, your communication may not be treated as privileged or confidential. Accordingly, please do not send us any information about any legal matter in which you are involved until you receive a written statement from us that we represent you. If you communicate with us by email or social media messaging in connection with a matter for which we already represent you, please remember that Internet email and social media are not secure and you should avoid sending sensitive, privileged, or confidential information by email and other electronic messages.

The best way to initiate contact with questions, comments, feedback, or concerns or to inquire about our legal services and what we can do for you is to call our office at [PHONE NUMBER].

Appendix D – Your Online Leads Ecosystem

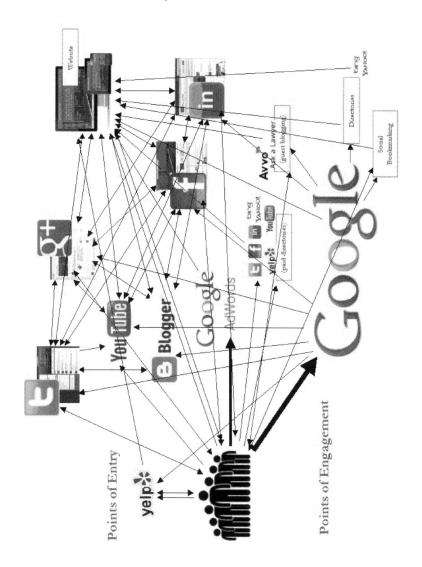

375

Appendix E – Examples of Google Remarketing Ads and Dimensions

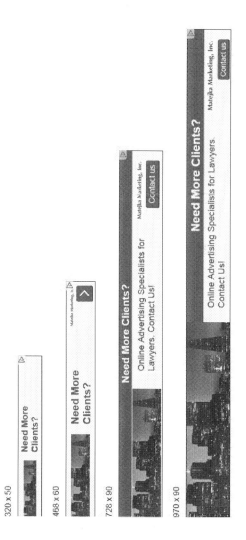

Appendix F – List of Directories

The following list of directories has been assembled over the years by my search engine optimization team. Directories fall into three general categories: national directories, legal directories and local directories. Below are national and legal directories that we have used. No list is included for local websites because it would be a difficult list to assemble for every city in the U.S.

Some of these directories are more valuable than others. Some are paid directories while others are free. There may be some on this list that no longer exist, and there may be new directories that are not listed here.

National Directories

Angie's List

Axciom

Better Business Bureau

Bing

BizJournals.com

Brownbook

ChamberofCommerce.com

CitySearch

CitySlick

CitySquares

CityVoter

Dex Media

Discover Our Town

EZ Local

Facebook

Foursquare

Get Fave

Google

Home Advisor

Hotfrog

Infignos

InfoUSA

InsiderPages

Judy's Book

Kudzu

LinkedIn

Local Site Submit

Local.com

Magic Yellow

Manta

Map Creator

MapQuest/Yext

Merchant Circle

MojoPages

My Huckleberry

ShowMeLocal

Superpages.com

TeleAtlas

Thumbtack

TripAdvisor

UsCity

USDirectory.com

Whitepages

Yahoo!

Yellowbook

Yellowbot

Yellowee

YellowPagesGoesGreen.org

Yelp

YP.com

Legal Directories

Allgoodlawyers

Alllocalsearch

Alphalegal.Com

Amacai

Attorney Rotary

Avvo

BestLawyers

Findlaw

Hg.org

Justia

LawInfo

Lawlink

Lawsuitwebsites

Lawyer.com

Lawyerfinder

Lawyers.com

Lead Counsel

Legalwebfinder

Washlaw

Wirelawyer

Appendix G - Schema Location Code

Law Firm Address Schema

Example:

Matejka Marketing, Inc.
77 Van Ness Avenue, Suite 101
San Francisco, CA 94102
Telephone: (415) 513-8736

```html
<div itemscope
itemtype="http://schema.org/LocalBusiness">

 <h2 itemprop="name"> Matejka Marketing,
Inc.</h2></b>

 <div itemprop="address" itemscope
itemtype="http://schema.org/PostalAddress">

 <div itemprop="streetAddress"> 77 Van Ness
Avenue, Suite 101</div>

 <span itemprop="addressLocality"> San
Francisco, </span><span
itemprop="addressRegion">CA </span><sp
an itemprop="postalCode">94102</span>
```

```
<div><Strong>Telephone: <span
itemprop="telephone">(415) 513-
8736</span></strong></div>
```

```
</div>
```

```
</div>
```


Law Firm Latitude/Longitude Schema

Look up your coordinates at
http://mygeoposition.com/

```
<div itemprop="geo" itemscope
itemtype="http://schema.org/GeoCoordinates">
```

```
<meta itemprop="latitude" content="37.7760190">
```

```
<meta itemprop="longitude" content="-
122.4199390">
```

```
</div>
```


Links to Complete Law Firm Schema:

https://schema.org/Attorney

End Notes

[1] http://searchengineland.com/googles-search-market-share-actually-dropping-237045

[2] It's noteworthy that even Yahoo's CEO chooses Google over her own search engine: "A presenter for shareholder proposals at [Yahoo's annual shareholders] meeting complained that links to bios for Yahoo board members didn't work, so [Yahoo CEO Marissa Mayer] Googled them — not exactly an endorsement for Yahoo Search."

http://blog.sfgate.com/techchron/2015/06/24/yahoos-marissa-mayer-gets-grilling-from-shareholders/

[3] BrightLocal Local Consumer Review Survey, 2017. https://www.brightlocal.com/learn/local-consumer-review-survey/

[4] 2015 Cone Communications/Ebiquity Global CSR Study. http://www.causemarketingforum.com/site/c.bkLUKcOTLkK 4E/b.6448703/k.BB16/Cone.htm

[5] It is recognized that not every legal service is purchased in a thin market, just as not every refrigerator is bought in an emergency setting. Perhaps a Sub Zero refrigerator is selected during a kitchen remodel after a thorough investigation of the alternatives. In the same way, a middle-aged daughter of an elderly parent in need of estate planning services may spend more time finding the attorney who is the best fit for her parent.

[6] The silhouettes of the lawyers as well as the call to action "request a lawyer" and "call us" are frozen to the bottom of the mobile site regardless of where the user scrolls or navigates. The silhouettes were added as visual interest to drop smart phone users' eyes to the call to action, with great effect.

[7] To be more precise, a "conversion" is when a Google user does one of the following things: (1) they clicked on one of your ads, came to your website, and used your contact form, (2) they saw your ad on a mobile device and clicked on your click-to-call icon that Google displays next to your ad under certain circumstances, or (3) they navigated to your website using their mobile device through one of your ads and clicked on one of your specially tagged click-to-call phone numbers.

[8] In this particular campaign, "Lawyers" is the name I happened to assign to the campaign wherein I'm targeting more general searches in the English language and "Spanish" is the name of the campaign in this account for all target phrases in the Spanish language.

[9] If you are in a sparsely populated area or if you practice an obscure area of law, it's possible that your traffic numbers are low because not many people are performing those searches. You may still have great visibility. There are reports to show where you rank in the search engines for your practice area's highest volume search terms, but this is beyond the scope of what we're discussing here.

[10] There is actually a fourth category of your ecosystem relating to search engine optimization. This fourth category is for activities that you do solely for purposes of helping the search engines locate you. The best example of this would be adding a listing for your law firm in a directory aggregator. It is not a supporting element, nor a point of engagement, nor an entry point because no person can view that information. Nonetheless, the listing is important because it helps Google establish your law firm in an exact physical location.

[11] Sheena S. Iyengar, Columbia University, and Mark R. Lepper, Stanford University. When Choice is Demotivating: Can One

386

Desire Too Much of a Good Thing? *Journal of Personality and Social Psychology, 2000, Vol. 79, No. 6, 995-1006*

[12] A "bounce" is when someone your website but quickly exits without viewing a second page. The "bounce rate" is a measure of how long people are your website's content. A low bounce rate of perhaps 40% suggests that people like your website because they're often moved to visit a second page on it. We discuss bounce rate more thoroughly in Chapter 5.

[13] 2012 heatmap study by TheLadders, as reported in *Business Insider*, May 23, 2012.

[Endnote removed]

[Endnote removed]

[16] http://www.comscore.com/Insights/Blog/Major-Mobile-Milestones-in-May-Apps-Now-Drive-Half-of-All-Time-Spent-on-Digital

[17] http://files.latd.com/Latitude-Next-Gen-Retail-Study.pdf

[18] http://searchenginewatch.com/sew/study/2343577/google-local-searches-lead-50-of-mobile-users-to-visit-stores-study

[19] A "conversion" is a term used to describe a legal consumer who has made contact with you through your website, whether through your contact form, mobile device, telephone, etc. The "conversion rate" is the percentage of consumers who make contact with you as a percentage of all consumers you have on your website. In the example above, a 25% conversion rate on the mobile version of your website indicates that 1 out of every 5 consumers who come to your website on their phones make contact with you.

[20] "Mobile devices with full browsers" is how Google describes hand-held mobile phones.

[21] Consider these numbers: Facebook: 1 billion users, 680 million daily users; YouTube: 4 billion video views per day; Google+: 400 million users; Twitter: 140 million users; and LinkedIn: 175 million users.

[22] University of Miami, School of Business Administration, March 2012.

[23] A complete set of remarketing banners and their dimensions for Google advertising is displayed in Appendix E.

[24] http://www.hbs.edu/faculty/Publication%20Files/13-070.pdf

[25] "Impression share" is a percentage of the number of times your ad shows as compared to the number of searches for which your ads are eligible to show. It is a rough measure of the amount of up-time your ads have over the course of a single day and is driven by your daily budget and the aggressiveness with which you bid.

[26] There are other reasons to advertise in social media other than lead generation. For example, you can run a Twitter campaign to increase your number of "Followers." In this instance, the advertising is used to increase Twitter as a supporting element and point of engagement to a larger of Followers.

[27] YouTube Press Room, https://www.youtube.com/yt/press/

[28] https://moz.com/blog/google-organic-clicks-shifting-to-paid

[29] "Usually" in this case means that when your ads show, they are usually in that spot. That is not to say that your ads necessarily "usually" run. Your "impression share" will determine how often your ads run as a percentage of when they are eligible to run. For example, if you have an impression share of 25%, then your ads will show 25% of the time that they are eligible to run. Even if your daily budget has not been exhausted and you're bidding on the Google user's search term, Google will display your ad only 1 out of 4 times. Ways to increase your impression share are largely a function of your daily budget and the aggressiveness of your bidding.

[30] Your daily budget can run all day if you set it so that Google shows your ads evenly over the day. Since most search activity occurs in the morning, we usually set the campaigns to "accelerated" which means that Google just shows your ads until your daily budget is exhausted. If your daily budget is low, you

may spend out by lunch time, but you had maximum visibility when it was most important to be visible, i.e., when searchers are more task-oriented.

[31] Although ironically, the top spot can sometimes result in a lower average cost per click than the second spot because the click through rate is so much better in the top spot resulting in a higher quality score.

[32] The term "long-tail search" refers to searches performed by Google users that are longer in length than the higher volume phrases. An example of a long-tail search may be "food poisoning personal injury lawyers downtown" rather than the much higher-volume search "injury lawyers."

[33] https://www.brightlocal.com/learn/local-consumer-review-survey/

[34] http://marketingland.com/app-store-ratings-a-single-star-jump-can-mean-340-percent-more-downloads-146744

[35] https://www.hbs.edu/faculty/Pages/item.aspx?num=41233

[36] In one study it was found that of the four largest websites containing attorney reviews, Yelp was most trusted by 61% of those surveyed. Study by Software Advice, October 2014.

[37] Keep in mind that Yelp calculates your star rating based only on the reviews that it has not filtered out of your profile. If you have 3 5-star reviews filtered out by Yelp and only one review that was not filtered out, then the star rating of that single review is your overall rating despite what the other reviewers said about you.

[38] ETHICS WARNING: Be mindful of the local rules of professional conduct when asking for reviews. As I read MRPC Rule 8.4, being too specific in what you want the reviewer to say could under some circumstances run afoul of restrictions against false or misleading communications.

[39] Naturally, be sure that the contacts to whom you reach out are former clients and if not, have them disclose in their review of

you that it is an endorsement, not a review. Otherwise, you may be violating the "false or misleading" communications prohibitions of RPC 7.1 (1-400 in California).

[40] If you're not sure whether you have Analytics in your website, here is how you check: Go to any page on your website, right-click the background of the page, and among your options, select "View page source" if you're using Chrome or Firefox; "View source" with Internet Explorer. This will display the code that renders that page on your website. "Find" (CTRL+F) and look for the word "analytics." If you do not see the word in your source code, chances are you do not have Analytics yet.

[41] You should consider outsourcing your Google advertising to a competent advertising manager. The learning curve for the advertising platform is steep, the build is labor intensive, and the cost savings in managing the account as well as your return on investment in an optimally performing campaign will more than pay for the setup and monthly management. I have overseen the delivery of over 1 billion law-related ads in Google and can speak to the complexity of the advertising medium.

[42] As of this writing, Google has been disabling Remarketing cookies for certain types of sensitive matters. So far, Google has disabled Remarketing for only two of our advertisers, both of them medical malpractice lawyer referral programs. Other medical malpractice Remarketing campaigns under our control continue to run, so it's unclear how Google intends to implement this new policy in the future. Our Google Policy Representative explained that the word "medical" on the lawyer referral programs' websites likely triggered the discontinuation in their cases.

[Endnote removed]

[44] View all of the CAN-SPAM requirements here: https://www.ftc.gov/tips-advice/business-center/guidance/can-spam-act-compliance-guide-business

45

http://www.abajournal.com/files/FO_477_REVISED_05_22_
2017.pdf

46 11 USCA 528(a)(4), but these cases speak to the disclaimer's
constitutionality: In re Reyes, 361 B.R. 276 (Bankr.S.D.Fla. Jan
17, 2007) and Milavetz, Gallop & Milavetz P.A. v. U.S., 355 B.R.
758 (D.Minn. Dec 07, 2006).

Made in the USA
Middletown, DE
12 April 2018